The McClellanville Coast
Seafood Cookbook

Dale Rosengarten

The McClellanville Coast *Seafood* Cookbook

More Recipes, Oral Histories, Poetry, Prose, Prints,
Photographs, and Paintings from McClellanville,
Awendaw, South Santee, Germanville, Tibwin, Seewee,
Buck Hall, Moss Swamp, and Honey Hill,
South Carolina

Edited by
Susan Williams

Published by
McClellanville Arts Council
McClellanville, South Carolina
1996

ISBN 1-882966-03-1

First printing, 1996.

Printed in the United States of America.

On the cover: Blue crabs at South Carolina Crab Company. Photograph by Bernadette Humphrey.

Table of Contents

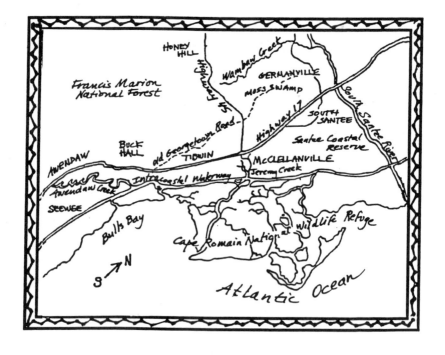

The McClellanville Coast

Introduction

Fish and shellfish have always been central to the lives of people along the southern Atlantic shore we call the "McClellanville Coast." As early as 8,000 years ago, Indians constructed huge rings of oyster shells mixed with the remains of conchs, mussels, clams, periwinkles, crabs, turtles, alligators, catfish, garfish, and drumfish. A European explorer, visiting a Sewee Indian settlement on Bulls Island in 1700, was served "oysters, conks, and clams" as well as "Turtle of several sorts." Another traveller was astonished by the "prodigious *Prawns*, and *Shrimps*," and the "Banks, nay Mountains of *Oysters* (some with Pearl) that seem to barocade the Cricks."

During the eighteenth and nineteenth centuries, rice and long-staple cotton, cultivated by workers of African ancestry, produced great wealth for a planter class that originated in the British Isles and France. Masters and slaves alike depended on the bountiful sea for their sustenance. After the demise, in this century, of the old staple crops, the territory between Awendaw Creek and the Santee River became a vegetable garden for distant urban markets. Today, commercial farming has nearly ceased along this stretch of coast, and most of the fields have reverted to pine. But one thing remains constant: the people's reliance on the produce of the sea.

A vibrant seafood industry is a mainstay of the local economy, while recreational fishing provides raw foods for the tables and freezers of creative cooks. In McClellanville we have oyster pie for Thanksgiving dinner, fresh shad roe at Easter, fish with grits for breakfast, crabmeat in our

7

deviled eggs, and shrimp in almost everything, including hushpuppies and potato salad. Even in hard times, no one goes hungry. Charles Williams recalls that during the Great Depression, "You had fish, you had shrimp, conch, oysters, clams, just from the sea. Mullet, flounder, spot, and an occasional striper, all caught with a net on a rising tide. You could take a mess of crabs on an oyster bank, with no bait—just the rake. You could eat all week and not double up."

In this cookbook you'll find directions for steaming shrimp, picking crab, filleting flounder, opening oysters, tenderizing conch, smoking mullet, stewing eel, dressing alligator, peeling and eating turtle. From classic church cookbooks come heirloom recipes like Pine Bark Fish Stew and Ladies' Aid Society Shrimp Pie. Delectable new dishes include McClellanville Caviar, Linguine with Shrimp, Artichokes, and Mushrooms, and Swordfish with Olive Sauce. For side dishes and desserts to complement the seafood, you will want to try Onion Kuchen, Fresh Herb Scones, Tomato Dumplings, and Fig Marmalade.

The McClellanville Coast Seafood Cookbook features tales of the sea by McClellanville residents William P. Baldwin, Gene Morrison, Charles Williams, Theodore Rosengarten, and Jay Shuler; memoirs by Dolly Gambrell and Sally Graham Vann; poems by J.O. McClellan, Irene Nuite Lofton, Mary Evelyn Lofton, and Sam Savage; paintings by Charles DeAntonio and Sally Cade; prints by Dale Rosengarten and her students; and photographs by Bernadette Humphrey and the members of Jenny Hane's 1994-95 SAIL class at St. James-Santee Elementary School, who also conducted interviews.

Adam Howard, Jeanne Edwards, and Frances Watson scouted for special recipes. Billy Dinwiddie interviewed netmaker Charles Williams. Barbara Dubiel, Olga Caballero, Martha Zierden, Bobbie McCutchen, Dale Rosengarten, Jackie Morrison, Becky Ashley, Judy Hierholzer, Marylou High, and other members of the Board of Directors of the McClellanville Arts Council collected recipes, proofed the text, and designed the cover. The women of New Wappetaw Presbyterian Church and McClellanville United Methodist Church graciously gave us permission to reprint several recipes from their cookbooks.

Alert readers will notice variant spellings of several words in this book—*Sewee* and *Seewee*, for example, *Dupre* and *DuPre*. In each instance, we have tried to conform to local custom rather than impose a standardized form. Thus *Seewee* is used when referring to the place, *Sewee* when referring to the Indian tribe.

This project was funded in part by an Expansion Arts grant from the Community Foundation and a Folk Arts grant from the South Carolina Arts Commission, as well as by donations from businesses and individuals. Proceeds from the cookbook support the activities of the McClellanville Arts Council, which sponsors classes, workshops, concerts, publications, and artist residencies in the schools.

Susan Williams
Executive Director

We would like to thank the following individuals and businesses for their generous financial assistance:

Patrons
Mr. and Mrs. Ralph C. McCullough
Mr. and Mrs. Peter Manigault
Dr. and Mrs. Paul H. Millar, Jr.
Mrs. Jane G. Skinner

Donors
Sheriff Al Cannon
Gedney Howe
McClellanville Civic Club
Dianne and Bony Peace
Mr. and Mrs. Michael Prevost
Gerald R. Tiller

Contributors
Robert D. Bibb
Dr. and Mrs. James B. Edwards
Betsey Geer
Edgar S. Jaycocks
McClellanville Telephone Company
J. Roger Rowe, M.D.
H. McRoy Skipper and Company
South Carolina Crab Company
Town of McClellanville

Friends
Randy and Claudia McClure

Sea Harvest

There was a time when only those
Who dwelt close to the shore
Were fortunate enough to have
These treats from ocean's store.
Their simple menus still remain
The best for me by far;
Much better they than those
Prepared with spices from afar.
Exalted chefs, exotic frills
And spices by the score
Are much like putting gilt on gold
And nothing but a show.

The hours of the day are
marked by the tidal flow,
And by the menus offered
The seasons we shall know.
Blue crabs we have in summer
The oyster winter fare
In spring the whelk is walking
A treat beyond compare.
The fall brings on the white shrimp
And winter's trout sublime
Regardless of the season,
There's seafood anytime.

The menus are unending
The catch I'm not so sure
We must be worthy stewards
The harvest to insure.

James O. McClellan, III

Rafael Rosengarten

Clusters
by William P. Baldwin

There are five bateaux and seven men. I know most of them at least by sight. Babe, I shrimped with, and Joe has been picking for the Ashleys a good many years. Junior is a mason's helper when he's not in the creek, so I know him from construction jobs. Marion Jenkins is the mason. He's put the foundations under and the chimneys in most of the homes around here for some years. That's not full-time work though. At least half of his income comes from picking oysters. I've been out of the creek a long time, and it's never really occurred to me that another generation would choose a life on the water. Three of the seven, though, are in their twenties.

The bateaux are linked bow to stern. Wooden barge-like boats, they are about twenty feet long and six wide, with squared-off bows. There's little art to them. Straight two-foot sides with no flair or bowing out at the belly. They've been built to last, built out of five-quarter rough pine, the seams caulked with roof tar and rope, battened over with plywood strips. At the bow a one-inch piece of line forms a bridle for towing. At the stern is the one concession to seamanship—the bateau rises over the final two feet to allow for a higher cutout for the small outboard.

Marion's partner is bolting the five-horse Evinrude into place. He straightens up and shakes my hand. His name is Snake, and he has a silver marijuana leaf stuck through one earlobe.

Marion takes charge of the hoodless, crankless two-cycle putter. He wraps a scrap of line around the flywheel, yanks it once. We are underway.

We all sit to the stern, but even this weight and a large piece of scrap iron isn't enough to bury the prop. The boat weighs at least a ton, and I suspect the bottom is painted with burnt motor oil. The other boats have vanished before we reach the first bend.

Marion swings the bateau in and runs it aground in the mouth of a small drain. Snake is already out, dropping an electric motor anchor off the bow. The stern anchor is a solid brass stuffing box. These will keep the bateau parallel to the shore.

Snake takes a wire bushel basket high up the bank and begins to fill it with long, narrow "blade" oysters. These he dumps in the middle of the boat. Marion takes a second basket and works close to the water's edge, picking up clusters that can be knocked into "singles." These are piled in the bow.

"Two or three together," he tells me. "Dem round oyster, that's what we can cull out." I'm familiar with this. I've made a halfway living off these same oysters along the water edge. Brown shelled, with sometimes a scrap of seaweed attached. Marion sends me along the bank to pick up. Rolling up his sleeves, he readies to get what's near the mouth of a drain, elbow deep.

The cluster oysters are culled on the bank. Most long blades bunch together, and come up with a small dagger of dead shell at the bottom. This is knocked off against another oyster and struck with a culling iron, a ten-inch piece of scrap iron in this case. Like cutting diamonds, only muddier.

Junior and his partner come around the bend and stop for a few minutes ahead of us, then come back and stop opposite on the far bank.

"We came here for scrap," Marion shouts across. "You and Bernard ain't like for scrap. You might as well go on from here."

"I like for scrap," Junior calls back. "Got to scrap today." But they crank up and head off, looking for something better. I've noticed we fishermen are always looking for something better, hoping to come around the bend of a drain and find thirty bushels of clean big oysters right at the bow. That's not likely to happen in March. Junior and Bernard were picking 120 bushels in this shore at Christmas. It's hard to come back here now and just "knock around dead shell."

Just below the water's edge is a conch. The musli-foot has come out and wrapped around an oyster. Marion wants him. "They good eating and they eat up on oysters bad." I pick up another a few yards further on. One of the boats had a couple dozen. I guess that can make a difference. Conchs and sponges are responsible in a large part for the absence of single oysters on these Awendaw creek bottoms.

Tide is turning as we approach a second small drain. I take out the basket of singles, bogging maybe fifty feet up the stream, pick up a good bushel from out of the three inches of clear water. When I was oystering, this is pretty much the way I worked, but Marion and Snake get what they get as close as possible to the boat. If they carry it's over a shell bank. They don't stop. Ever.

Marion announces a move. We climb in, crank up, and slip along the edge of the creek bank. Snake picks up the wide, short-handled shovel and begins to separate the single pile from the clusters. This done, he joins Marion in watching the banks. I never used to work the flood tide for more than a few minutes, but Marion announces our day's not half done. We slow, confer. Marion checks his watch. The bateau turns in. Only a couple of feet of bank shows now above the flood tide. We'll be pulling up blades and tossing them into the boat right beside us. An hour ago this was boggy bottom that we would have had to cross. Now everything's at arm's length.

"Anything too small, let 'em go," Marion calls. "Don't want to ruin the top of you boat." We've got some decent oysters already in the boat, and we don't want to make them look bad by putting trash on top.

A tug passes in the cut. Five hours of steady picking and Marion announces we're done. Only one other boat is still out, and it shows up while we're tying into place. We've done better than most—should have with three workers. Still Marion estimates only about forty bushels of clusters and five or six singles. At Christmas Marion was doing that well by himself, but there's no complaint. The outboard comes off and is stored on deck.

 *Clusters*

Forty bushels. That's five better than the best day I had in the two winters I picked. It's twice what I usually brought in. But there were crewmen then picking 100 bushels a day, day after day. Last year there were some still doing that well, and if things turn around they'll be doing it again next winter. Marion says he'll be retired by then. Same here.

Shrimping Fever
by Gene Morrison

Shrimping fever entered my blood at an early age. I could recognize a boat coming into our harbor by the sound of its exhaust. I knew who the pilot was, the size of net it pulled, and how many pounds of shrimp it caught. Hanging around the docks after school was a pastime for many boys. We had fish-catching contests and listened to tales of the sea, trying to imagine the old sailing schooners and freight boats.

Sometimes we would rig a bateau with sails made of burlap bags or an old sheet. Anything that resembled a pole was used for a mast. It took one boy to steer with an oar while two held the mast in position and another bailed the boat. Evenings after school we paddled to an oyster bank and used yard rakes to pull oysters from deeper water

onto the creek banks so they could be gathered. We sold them to a local oyster shucking house for a dollar a bushel.

Early spring is time for boats and nets to be cleaned and repaired. Marine yards pulled the larger boats ashore for bottom repairs. Smaller boats were moored at high tide on sand bars along the edge of the creek. When the tide went out, one side of the bottom was exposed. Repair work had to be done rapidly because it would be only six hours before the tide returned. Afterward a layer of dry pinestraw was placed along the keel. Burning the straw dried the planks enough for antifouling paint to adhere. On the following day, this procedure was repeated on the other side.

Whenever a boat mast cracked or rotted, a cypress tree from one of the swamps was used to replace it. The bark was removed and the new mast was outfitted with hardware from the old one. A silver dollar was placed under the foot for good luck.

Netmakers would build new nets using cotton webbing, then dip them into a tar vat. Working with freshly dipped nets in the sunshine, a fisherman's arms and face would blister.

During the fall shrimp run, boats from North Carolina sometimes showed up. They were always well maintained, so clean and white. Their nets were clean and white, too, dipped in a solution of lime and salt water instead of tar. Visiting crewmen were always barefooted, young and old alike. Some squawked like sea birds, some meowed like cats, and others would talk so fast a highway patrolman's radar couldn't catch their words.

Every evening I'd watch boats come in and unload their catch. The docks were humming with activity. At last Daddy said that I could go shrimping.

Shrimpers rise at about three in the morning to start their day's work. A two-hour late start can result in a poor catch. Going to bed early wasn't any problem, but getting to sleep was impossible. I lay there wondering what the following day would bring. It wasn't long before Daddy was tapping my shoulder, whispering to be quiet. When I eased out of bed and went into the living room, I saw him sitting there with a cigarette in one hand and a cup of coffee in the other. Children were not allowed to drink coffee. Mama made me some hot water tea. She put two spoons of sugar into a cup and poured in boiled water. When the cup was half full she added milk from a can.

Mama's cigarette had now burned about half its length. She would never thump the ashes off, just let them fall whenever, wherever, and brush them off her dress.

Very seldom did a car pass so early in the morning. Only an occasional dog barking broke the morning stillness. We heard the squeak of bucket handles and the scrape of loose rock as Daddy's crew passed the house on their way to work.

Picking up his bucket, which held our alarm clock, some cigarettes, and biscuits filled with fried fatback for lunch, Daddy said, "It's time to go." I carried a jug of iced tea to drink during the day.

There were oak trees along both sides of the street, their branches interwoven to form a dark tunnel. Moonlight could not shine through the thick branches. We headed for a dim street light ahead on the corner. Now the squeaks and the scraping sounds were coming from

Daddy's bucket and shoes. I was barefoot, and I stumped my toes on the uneven pavement. Daddy's cigarette gave a glow every time he dragged on it.

On the docks, a few stray cats were searching for a meal. Daddy's crew were manhandling 300-pound blocks of ice onto the boat. "Got the little cap'n, eh?" they said. "Train 'em right."

Daddy stored our lunch in the cabin and started making coffee. The pot was black with soot, with a yellow stain around its rim. He held it upside down and banged it against a railing, dumping yesterday's grinds. After a brief rinse, he filled it with water, and shook in a handful of grinds.

After getting his coffee cooking, Daddy serviced the engine. He put a little gasoline in the primer cups and pulled on the cranking bar. After several tries, the engine turned over and ran smoothly with a steady popping sound.

Daddy signaled the crew to cast off. "Cap, we got um trow off," one crewman shouted. We passed other boats still moored at the dock without any activity. "Dey ain't know whea we bin now," a crewman remarked. I'd heard tales that Daddy would sometimes leave earlier than usual to slip away from the others. Some joked he wouldn't crank the engine, just drift out with the ebb tide, pushing with a pole.

Daddy knew every mud flat, creek, and shortcut through the marshes. I sat as far forward as possible on the bow trying to understand our route. Looking back toward the pilot house, I could see our navigating lights as a dim glow coming through the mist of our exhaust.

Daddy's crew sat on the stern, their heads nodding, trying to catch a nap. As we neared the ocean, first rays of sun were beginning to brighten the sky. A school of porpoise followed our net, catching fish as they washed through the mesh. Hundreds of gulls dived into our wake.

Shrimpers could not drag at random. There were too many obstructions to snag the nets or load them with coral rocks. They checked bottom samples and water depth with a sounding lead tied to a small rope. On the bottom end of the lead was an indentation containing some Octagon soap. When the soap hit bottom it would pick up mud or sand. You hoped it was mud. Sand usually meant you were close to rocky bottom.

During cold winter months Daddy would gill net fish to squeeze by until shrimp season. We used a twenty-foot bateau with a pair of oars for power. The net was about two hundred yards long and twelve feet deep. The webbing was fine as hair.

We left before dawn to work a low tide. A light glaze of ice covered the net. My job was to row the bateau and not make any noise. Daddy's was to study the water for signs of fish.

Suddenly Daddy would spot some movement and throw the net pole, which stuck in the mud at the edge of the marsh. I quietly rowed away, parallel to the shore. Then we bumped and made noise to spook the fish into the net.

We pulled on the net until our hands were so cold we could no longer feel the webbing. I always had on tennis shoes. There was never enough money to buy rubber boots for children.

It was always depressing to return home after a bad day's fishing. Daddy would sit staring into the fireplace, poking the fire with a stick. On cold windy nights a draft coming through our house would swing the ceiling light. We would often put water in our refrigerator to keep it from freezing.

One day someone offered Daddy a deal—work a boat and pay along, not going through a bank. This boat didn't have any machinery to handle the nets or the catch. Some of the planks were wormeaten and needed replacing. That didn't matter. We were happy with our boat, my daddy, my two brothers, and me. Holes in the raggy net could be tied shut with string. We could pump the bilge with a manual pump if the leaks didn't get any worse.

They got worse. Daddy would wake me up at night to go stoke the pump. Soon someone was pumping almost all the time. We put the boat on a sand bar and pushed cotton into the holes, covering them with roofing tar. It cut down on the pumping. But one day when we were at sea, without another boat in sight, the bilge started filling. We pumped away, but could not stay ahead of the rising water. Daddy discovered that a plank was about to fall off the bottom of the boat. He grabbed a blanket and stuffed it in the hole. We pulled in our net and headed for home, trying not to wash out the blanket.

Daddy steered the boat and made a fish stew while we took turns at the pump. Soon we smelled gas in the bilge—our gas tank has rusted through. Now it was a race between sinking and running out of gas.

Our engine shut off as we approached the dock. Daddy pulled the boat up on a mud flat and we watched it fill with water. A summer of excitement and dreams had come to an end.

Nico Sardet

Junior Did It

An interview with Charles Williams, netmaker, Buck Hall

I'm a quick study. I walk by a guy and see him do something and I can turn around and do it too. With my father, that's the only way I had to learn to make nets. He always did it in the dining room right on the wall, by the buffet. He had a nail up there, and that's where the net would hang. When he's not doing anything, especially at night, he'll come in and knit for a couple of hours. He's pulling it down, tauting it, knottin', knottin'.

Of course I'm right there looking at him, every time. When he finishes sewing he says, "Boy, don't mess with this net." He'd only tell you something once. That's all he'd *have* to tell you. One time. "Boy, don't mess with this net." All he did was say "Boy!" And you better not run. Between my daddy and mama, you could see them coming with a stick as big as this house. And if you run they going to kill you. The best thing you can do was just stand there and say, "I didn't do it." But you know they going to beat you anyway.

My sister Ann and the other kids would run by the net and shake it, and I'd go by, you know, gettin' used to the way it looked. And finally, I got the nerve and said, "I bet I can sew just like Daddy." Well, *that* was a mistake. I sewed, but it wasn't like Daddy's. I got a good tail cuttin' for that, and then, of course, I was still watchin' him, and then one day he says, "Sit down here." He was in the middle of a net. I was nine or ten years old. Quick as I was, it still took me several months to learn how to tie all them knots.

Most families then had two nets. You had a mullet net, and then you had what we call a "poor man net," 'cause nothin' get out of that. The only thing get out of that one was water, sandy water. You used the mullet net strictly for mullet—it would let the little boys go and keep the big ones. The shrimp net didn't let anything go. You could catch a million mullet with one cast. You could catch you a tub full.

Daddy would take us fishing twice a year, me and my sister Ann and my younger brother Biddie. His right name was James—me they called Junior. Every year Daddy would get a piece of stiff wire and a pole. When we see that, we *know* we going crabbing.

Daddy would make a dip net out of a piece of old chicken wire. We used to get bull lip from Mr. Walter Shepard—he was a professional crabber, with trot lines. You could buy that stuff by the barrel. We'd go out on low tide, crab, and then when the tide got up he'd go and cast for mullet. Once, when we were coming back in there was an old garfish—never saw one in my life. The old man says, "Look at that fish!"

We all look—*Oooh!*"

The old man says, "I'm going to get that joker."

He took that oar, turned it on its side. And he chopped him—*what cha!* Water went everywhere. He throwed the oar down, and grabbed the dip net. "I think I got him!"

He stuck that dip net just as far as he could reach in the water, and he brought it up, and there's the biggest and the ugliest damn fish you want to see. That scared us. He'd hit it right across the back with that oar; he just reached in there and pulled it up. Lordy, Lordy.

We took it home. People say, "Ooooh, Charles got a *garfish*." They got it out of the net, and that daggone thing cut their tail. But they got it clean, and that was the worst-tasting fish—mealy, just as white as a cotton ball.

My grandmother would send us to the DuPre's pond to see if we could find any cooter. For those who don't know, that's a yellow-belly freshwater turtle.

We used to run up and down the pond, me, my sister, and Biddie. I used to get beat for everything, because "Junior did it." They did it, too, but when the pressure come, *Junior* did it. And old Junior stick right there and get a tail cuttin'. But one day we went back there, and they used to tell us, "Walk the bank and see if ya'll see any yellow-bellied cooters." And we would get out and walk the bank. Lookin' for the cooters laying their eggs, or one close that we could get. We go out there, we found a couple nests, with little eggs, you know, 'bout the size of your thumbnail. Take the eggs home, wash them up, cook them. We'd pinch a hole in them, like the big sea turtle eggs, but these were small.

So one day we were out there, we must have caught about four of them big old yellow-bellied cooter, put 'em in a sack and took 'em home. And the people sitting there said, "Boy, don't let that turtle bite you—it never turn loose till thunder roll." And they go, "How you gonna kill it?" My grandaddy says, "Come here and lemme show you." Got a doggone sharp stick and rammed it in.

Sometimes they get a pliers or a hook and stretch the head out and chop it off. *"Now* what you gone do with it?" Got this big old pot of water, hot water, put him in it, peel him. Cut the legs off, cut the shell off, cut the meat in squares, clean it, take the guts out, salt and pepper it, throw it in the pot. Steam him up.

The yellow-belly turtle's skin is black, but it has a yellow stripe in it. Sucker cook up just as pretty. We could really chomp on it.

One day Junior decided to *really* catch some cooters. Had a hoe fork stick, put a twenty-penny nail in it, bent it with the head. That thing was maybe five-and-a-half, six feet long. And they didn't lie on me this time. *Junior* did this.

We got down there to the pond O.K. Then Sister and Biddie says, "What we do now, Junior?"

"We can roll up our pants and walk the pond."

"What if a alligator come?"

"Got this sharp stick with a nail on it."

Got on out in the pond.

"Junior, what we gone do now?"

"If you ever feel something hard, call me."

Sister call me: "I got my foot on something!"

So I go down there, you know, put my foot on top of hers, say, "Pull your foot out!" And I run my hand down there and feel, "Oh yeah, that's a cooter!"

You know with cooters, the head part is smooth, and the tail end it got those saw teeth. So I put my hand on my foot, and I go back, and when I feel a sharp end, I grab from that end, 'cause the smooth end is the head, and you don't want to grab that. *Big* old joker. Throw it in the sack. We go right along, until we got about seven of them. Got 'em in the sack. We come up and there's a hole at the side of the bank, under the top of the water. Red and yellow dirt was spread around, which meant it was a deep hole.

"What live in there, Junior?"

"That's a *alligator* hole."

"What if they be in there?"

I get that stick with the nail and ram that stick in that hole like I *knew* what I was doing.

"They ain't must be in there, Junior!"

I say, "Well, let's go."

So we made our way to the hill. Water ain't more than two feet deep. Now when we got up there, the talk was, we can't tell *no body* we been in the pond. So we all got together and made a pact, told this thing, you know, "Cross my heart and hope to die, I will never tell."

Everybody did that, the three of us—me, my sister, and Biddie. "I swear." We dragged that sack home, and time we hit the front yard, Biddie yelled out, "Mama, them chillen been in that pond!"

Them chillen. *He* wasn't in there. They come running out. And the only thing that saved us was they saw that sack of cooter we had, and that's how I got out of that one. They thought we had better sense than to go in that pond. Little did they know. The Good Lord had to be with us that day. They was huge alligators in that place. What would have happened if that bad boy was home?

27

Keep in mind, all I had was a twenty-penny nail drove into the end of a hoe fork stick.

◆◆◆◆◆

One thing I didn't do—you didn't have to beat me for it—was swimming. We went to the dock one time, supposedly to fish. *Supposedly.* Everybody could swim except Junior. But old Junior was smart. Don't let anybody fool you now, Junior's a smart fellow. Junior knew he couldn't swim, but Junior wanted to go in the water. What did Junior do? Junior got on one of these fellow's shrimp boats, got a rope, and tied it round his waist. Dive over. *Ple-tu-choww.* If Junior can't swim, all Junior got to do is pull himself in.

Well, I don't know how long I was under, but somebody pulled me in. What I forgot about is all that loose slack. Ain't nobody had to kill me. I tried to kill myself!

Never. Never. *Never* after that day. Never *once* did I go in that water and say I'm gonna swim.

My buddies and I used to go up on the buoys that you see in the inland waterway. They would swim up to the buoy, climb up to the top, and dive under, *Plu-chow.* "Come on, Junior."

"Heck no, I ain't lost nothin'," I'd say.

One of my buddies named Cat who claimed he could swim pretty good, he went up on that daggone buoy and when he dived off that sucker, he must have buried his head in two feet of mud and anchor. Ho! And we had to drag him out of there, but he didn't die, you know. He had a good cut. While we were getting him back home, we

went by a ditch that connects the inland waterway to the big pond on Dupre Road. Every once in a while, I'd see a crab swim by in the ditch. There were five or six of us going along. I was the only one seen the crabs, and I didn't tell the others. You got your little secret too, you know. When I got home I said, "Hey, look here, Sister, you and Biddie get the rake and tub—we goin' crabbin'!"

No bait, just an iron yard rake. Went back to that same spot in the ditch. We sat there, and every crab came by, we took that rake and drug him out the water. We raked them jokers as they come by. Don't you know when we left we had a tub full of crab. There were some cedars along the bank. We put some cedar branches on top to keep 'em from running off. Then when we got to the woods, we got to a moss oak tree, and pulled the moss off it, stacked it on, and brought it on home. I never seen so much of meat in a crab as those crabs come out of that brackish water.

Another fish story. Me and a couple friends of mine used to "borrow" our fathers' nets, to show that we were growing up. It was me, a guy named Danny, and the guy we called Cat. Man, we went down to the dock, right where Weewa's dock is now. On the other side, across the river, was an old building. In the water was a eat-out shell of a boat, just the stern part of a boat, with three sides. We rowed out there with an old shovel and a piece of board, you know, and got over there. *Boontcha, boontcha, boontcha.* When we got over there we got out, running up and down on the bank looking for clam and stuff, and there's these three porpoises just running as far as they can come around this old eat-out hull.

"Hot damn, boys, if we could get over there!"   So we got back in the boat and pushed off. We done figgered that porpoise eat fish. There got to be some mullet over there, 'cause they just got the water sudsin'–*schowp, schowp, schowp, schowp.* So we eased the boat over there, eased over, and of course when we get up to the thing, the porpoise is gone.

Junior took the cast net, throw it inside that old hull, and *"Oh, shucks! Oh, shucks!"*   Couldn't curse then. *"Oooh, shucks!"*

"What's the matter, Junior?"

"I think I got Daddy's net hung!"

We pulled, and the fellows said, "No, it can't be hung too bad."

"How's that?"

"Cause it's *moving* a little bit." We pulled on it a little bit, and it moved. We kept pulling it, and it moved. The boat got up against the two sides, and we pulled on it, and it moved. And we just kept on pulling.

We had a net full of fish. *Net full* of fish. That's why it wouldn't move! All you could see was eyes and teeth. "Boy, we got the fish! We got the fish!"

And we divided it up in the usual way, one for you and one for me, to make sure nobody got no more than the other. And we got home, and Daddy says, "Where you caught them fish?"

"That old boat."

"Ya'll been cross the creek?" Hot damn. He didn't beat us, but he says he doesn't want to find us down there no more. And we came home, and that was the end of that.

•••••

At Drayton Hall, I'm a crafts demonstrator. I sit down and start netting. People come by and look at me, and ask how I do it, how long I been doing it, who taught me, and all this.

And up walks this guy—at first I thought he was drunk. Grabs the net, and he looks at me. He say, "Yeah, you think you slick."

And I say, "'Scuse me?"

"You think you slick."

And I say, "What do you mean?"

"Man can't make nothin' like this. Not from no one piece of cord like that." I'm sitting there netting, making the net, yet he says a man can't do it.

And he says, "I know what you done—you found a big old mesh material, and you found a way to cut it, put it together, make a net out of it. You can't do that." He says, "I'll tell you what, I'll bet you five dollars I'll find out how you did it. I'm going to find out how you did it, and I'm going to show you, you ain't going to kid me. I'm going to find out how you done it."

I got him a chair, and I said, "You want the net with the bullet on it, or you want the naked net?"

He says, "Give me the one with the bullet on it. That's the finished one, and I'm going to find it."

And that joker sat there and went over every knot. Over thirteen thousand knots in this net, and he went from one string to the other. "You ain't going to shit me, I'm going to find it. I'm going to find it." And when it was headed toward three hours, I looked at the chair and the chair was there, and he wasn't there—he done gone. So I guess he didn't find what he thought I'd done.

You know when you buy a net out the store, you look at it close and they're all cut. Especially Japanese nets, they're cut in pieces, and then sewed like material. That's why they open funny. That's what he thought I had done. But mine are handmade, and you can look all day and all you would find is an occasional knot, and if you don't look close enough you ain't going to find that knot. He took off—I think his feelings was a little hurt. I had a ball with him.

It's all right to say it can't be done, but if you're sitting there right in front of them . . . .

Will Bigelow

How to Buy and Handle
Fresh Fish and Shellfish

Whole Fish

Look for bright, clear eyes and gills that still show redness. If the eyes are cloudy or the gills are brown, the fish is not fresh. The skin should also look fresh and bright, not gray or faded. It should bounce back if you press it with your finger. The only odor should be a faint smell of seaweed. Never buy a fish that smells strong.

Generally speaking, one pound of small whole fish will feed one person. One pound of large whole fish will go a bit further, especially if it is stuffed. For example, a three to three-and-a-half pound stuffed fish will serve three to four people.

Fish Steaks and Fillets

These should look clear and translucent, not milky and white. They should feel firm and moist to the touch, not dry or spongy. If you run your finger over the surface of a fillet, it should remain clean. For fish fillets, steaks, and kabobs, allow seven to eight ounces per person. Choose the freshest fish available. If your recipe calls for flounder but the grouper is fresher, buy the grouper.

Oysters and Clams

Shells should be tightly closed. If any are slightly open, touch them gently. If they do not close tightly when touched, they should be discarded, as should any that float in water or have broken shells. Scrub shells with a stiff brush under cold water. To make opening easier, hammer off a small section of the flat shell at the unhinged edge. Wearing gloves, force a thin, strong knife into the hinge. Turn the knife to pry the upper shell loose. Cut through the hinge muscle at the back. Run the knife between the shells to open.

Poaching Oysters

In a skillet, bring two cups of water and half a teaspoon of salt to a boil. Add one cup of shucked oysters. Lower heat and simmer for four to six minutes. Do not overcook. Oysters are done when their edges begin to curl.

Mussels

To test mussels for freshness, try to slide the halves together. If they budge, discard as "mudders"—they're full of mud. Wash in running water and scrub with a stiff brush. Clip the "beards" with scissors.

Crabs

Whole crabs spoil quickly if not cared for properly. Buy only living crabs and cook them before removing the meat from the shell. If kept at temperatures below 50°, they may be dormant. Warm them up slowly and check for signs of life. If there is any doubt about whether they are alive, do not cook them.

Boiling Crabs

Bring eight quarts of water and two tablespoons salt to a boil. Wash crabs in cool water. Place two or three at a time in boiling water and cook about eight minutes per pound.

Shrimp

Pull the legs to one side and peel off the shells. Run a knife or other sharp object down the outside curve to remove the dark "sandbag." To boil shrimp in the shell, use a quart of water and a tablespoon of salt for every pound of shrimp. Bring water to a boil and drop in the shrimp. Turn down the heat and simmer for three minutes, or until the shrimp turn pink.

Squid

The pouch, the tentacles, and the two fins are edible. The skin, the pen, the head, and the beak have to be removed. Rinse squid in cold water and pull out the pen, a hard, shell-like protrusion located inside the rim. Discard the pen. Gently separate the head and the body. The entrails should come out in one piece. Pull off the mottled skin from the pouch and the fins. Cut the tentacles off the head just below the eyes. Discard the head. Reach inside the tentacles to squeeze out the hard beak. Discard the beak.

Conch

Freeze conchs in the shell for at least twenty-four hours. Thaw completely. With a fork, pull whole conch out of shell. Using a brush or knife under running water, clean off the black parts. Cut light meat from conch and discard the rest. Tenderize light meat with mallet, then cut in small pieces.

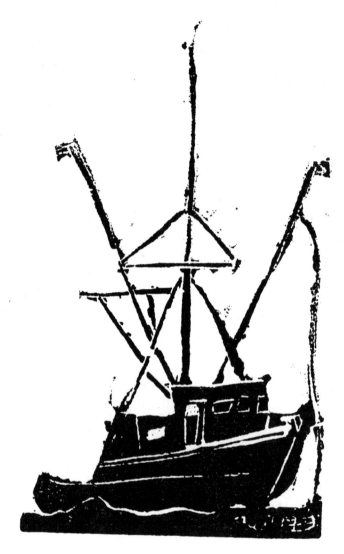

Bochét Leland

Appetizers

I grew up in a oyster factory down there in Buck Hall. We had over a hundred head of women picking the oyster out the shell. That's all we had to depend on, men and women—the oyster factory. I used to work in the picking room. Later on, they had a big machine that shuck the oysters. A white man named George Davis made that machine in the '50s. He made it out of tin, like a big wide boiler. The force of the water whooshed the oyster out the shell. The water been up like that—pour down. We were sorry when it happen. So much women lose their job. I didn't lose my job—I was working the packing room.

Georgia Bryant

McClellanville Caviar
(Shrimp and Black Beans)

16 oz. cooked black beans (canned are okay)
¼ cup finely chopped peppers
½ cup chopped red onion
2 Tbs. chopped cilantro
2/3 cup picante sauce or salsa
¼ cup lime juice
Salt to taste
2 Tbs. honey
2 Tbs. vegetable oil
1½ lbs. cooked shrimp, chopped

Toss all ingredients. Cover and chill for 8 hours, stirring occasionally. Serve with crackers as an appetizer or on a bed of lettuce as a salad.

Bernadette Humphrey

Shrimp Mold

1 can condensed tomato soup
1 cup mayonnaise
1 small package cream cheese
1 packet Knox gelatin
1 cup cooked shrimp, chopped
½ cup chopped onion
½ cup chopped celery

Mix gelatin in 2 Tbs. cold water and heat until dissolved. Add mayonnaise, cheese, and gelatin to warmed tomato soup and stir until smooth. Add shrimp, onion, and celery; mix well. Pour into a greased mold and chill until firm. Serve with crackers.

Bobbie Davis

Hot Crab Dip

1 stick butter
8 Tbs. flour
A dash of curry powder
4 cups milk or diluted evaporated milk
1 lb. crabmeat
A dash of each of the following: celery salt, onion salt, salt,
    and black pepper

Melt butter in a heavy pot. Stir in flour and curry powder.
Add milk, cooking on moderate heat, stirring until thick.
Add crabmeat and remaining seasonings. Serve hot with
crackers or heap in small pastry shells.

Judith Fortner

Aunt Blanche's Hot Crab Dip

8 oz. cream cheese, softened
1 small onion, grated
2 Tbs. milk
Salt and pepper to taste
8 oz. fresh crabmeat
Sliced almonds

Combine softened cream cheese, onion, milk, salt, and pepper. Add crabmeat, stirring just enough to mix. Spread mixture into baking dish. Top with sliced almonds. Bake at 350° for 15 to 20 minutes or until bubbly. Serve hot with wheat thins.

Gloria Squires

Bet's Crab Dip

1 cup crab meat
1¼ cup grated sharp cheddar
½ cup mayonnaise
4 Tbs. French dressing
1 tsp. horseradish
Juice of ½ lemon

Mix all ingredients and refrigerate. Serve with crackers or chips.

Lyda Graham

Rafael Rosengarten

Chilled Crab Dip

8 oz. cream cheese
½ cup mayonnaise
2 oz. cheddar cheese, finely grated
1 small clove garlic, grated
1 tsp. Worcestershire sauce
1 Tbs. finely grated onion
2 Tbs. French dressing
8 oz. crabmeat
Salt and pepper to taste

Bring cream cheese to room temperature; beat until soft. Add all other ingredients and mix well. Shape into a mold or serve in a dish. Chill several hours before using.

Bobbie Davis

Crab Paté

1 can cream of mushroom soup, undiluted
1 envelope unflavored gelatin
3 Tbs. cold water
¾ cup mayonnaise
8 oz. cream cheese, softened
1 small onion, grated
1 cup finely chopped celery
½ lb. fresh crabmeat

Heat soup in a saucepan over low heat. Stir in cream cheese. Dissolve gelatin in cold water and add to soup mixture. Add remaining ingredients. Grease a 4-cup bowl or gelatin mold and spoon in mixture. Chill until firm. Unmold and serve with assorted crackers.

Gloria Squires

Deviled Crab Eggs

1 dozen chilled, hard-boiled eggs
8 oz. crabmeat
1 cup mayonnaise
2 Tbs. fresh lemon juice
½ tsp. fresh dill
Black pepper

Cut cooked eggs in half lengthwise. Remove yolks.
Combine mayonnaise, lemon juice, dill, and pepper. Add
crabmeat and stir. Fill egg halves with mixture and chill.
Sieve yolks and sprinkle a small amount over each egg.

Bernadette Humphrey

Smoked Fish Spread

Crumble any variety of smoked fish. Mix mayonnaise, a
small amount of grated onion, a dash of garlic powder or
garlic salt, and a few drops of Tabasco. Adjust to taste.
Fold in fish and chill. Good served with wheat thins.

Shirley McClellan

Salmon-Stuffed Pumpernickel

½ lb. smoked salmon
1 8-oz. package light cream cheese
3 green onions
2 tsp. Worcestershire sauce
2 Tbs. fresh lemon juice
½ cup low fat milk
½ tsp. Tabasco
¼ cup capers, drained
1 round loaf pumpernickel bread

Put first 7 ingredients into food processor and blend until smooth. Cover and refrigerate until ready to serve. Cut off the top of the round loaf of pumpernickel and hollow it out. Fill with salmon mixture; top with capers. Serve with cocktail bread.

Ellen Saum

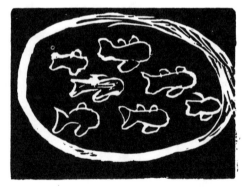

Hopi Savage

Deborah's Stupendous Oysters Rockefeller

1 lb. bacon, diced
1 package frozen chopped spinach
1 can sliced water chestnuts, minced finely
Juice of ¼ lemon
2 tsp. lemon pepper
2 tsp. Cajun seasoning
1 Tbs. Worcestershire sauce
2 dozen large oysters, shucked
1 package Knorr Béarnaise sauce mix, prepared
¼ cup butter
1 cup milk

In a skillet, fry bacon very crisp. Drain excess grease. Add spinach, water chestnuts, lemon juice, spices, and Worcestershire sauce. Place oysters in half-shells on baking sheet. Top with 2 Tbs. spinach mixture and 1 to 2 Tbs. Béarnaise sauce. Bake at 350° for 20 minutes. Serves 4 to 6. Even people who don't like oysters will like this!

Oven Roasted Oysters

Preheat oven to 500°. Wash oysters and place on a broiler pan. Roast in oven for 10 to 15 minutes or until shells pop open.

Betsy Hansen

Opening Oysters, Jackie's Way

Stop up the sink. Pour boiling water over oysters. The shells will open a little bit. Drain the water and shuck with an oyster knife. It helps to wear gloves, but I never do!

Jackie Morrison

Fried Oysters

Have a hot griddle, cover it with butter, have a dish of grated crackers, dip the oysters in the crackers, one by one, and place them singly on the griddle, fry until brown on both sides and serve while hot. Many prefer them cooked this way to any other.

from an old clipping discovered by Dolly Gambrell

Sewee Shell Ring, Late Archaic Period (5,000 to 3,000 years ago)

Located in the Francis Marion National Forest off Salt Pond Road and listed in the National Register of Historic Places, the Shell Ring, also known locally as "Spanish Fort," can be reached by a mile-long interpretive hiking trail.

The Late Archaic Indians were the seaside clans of a great family of river people, known by ethnologists as Siouans. They harvested and ate fish and shellfish, depositing the remains in rings and middens which are still visible along the coast. The rings provide archaeological evidence of a sedentary, or permanent, village; coastal Indians before and after this time lived in temporary camps, moving seasonally to the interior to hunt deer and gather nuts and berries. Despite the fact that much shell was removed over the years to surface roads and make lime, the Sewee Shell Ring is more than one hundred feet across and ten feet high in spots. The average length of oyster shells deposited in the mound is 4.29 inches, almost twice the size of living oysters currently found in the area.

Mr. Kobylenski's Clams

Shuck clams after putting them in the freezer for a short time. If they are small, 1 to 1½", leave them whole and put them back into half shells. Chop larger clams coarsely. Sprinkle with bread crumbs and ½ tsp. catsup. Top each with a small piece of bacon. Run under the broiler until bacon is done and clams are bubbly. They can also be cooked on the grill, covered with foil.

Dolores Humphrey

I live in a house
By the water's edge
Not far from the open sea,

And I like to pretend
As the boats go by
That they belong to me.

Today I would sail the ocean wide
Tomorrow the rivers I'd roam—
I'd gather treasures from every land
And sail with them back home.

Mary Evelyn "Teen" Lofton, 1905-1992. *Verses at Random.*

Willie's Lobster Wraps

2 lbs. pre-cooked lobster meat
½ lb. bacon

Cut lobster into 2" pieces. Wrap each lobster chunk with a 3" strip of bacon. Broil on broiling pan until lightly browned, then turn and broil other side.

Willie Humphrey

Virdell Mercer

Willie's Lobster Dip

3-4 lobster tails, ½ lb. each
1 Tbs. parsley
1 Tbs. garlic salt
1 tsp. black pepper
1 Tbs. dillweed
2 Tbs. horseradish
1/8 cup mayonnaise
1/8 cup sour cream
Juice from ½ lemon

Steam lobsters and remove from shells. Shred lobster meat in a blender or food processor until fine, combining remaining ingredients. Garnish with paprika, parsley, and lemon slices.

Willie Humphrey

In the McClellanville of my childhood, everybody was known by a relationship. I was not related by blood to the rest of the village. Neither was my grandmother and, although my grandmother was cousin to Cousin Archie's cousin, we were set apart by this. So I spent many hours in the kitchen with my grandmother's cook, Urcile, listening to gospel songs on her radio and talking about God and sugar ants. Uncle Swinton didn't like the noise of the radio, and was constantly asking my grandmother to ask Urcile to turn it down. He loved and sang the old Gullah spirituals but could not abide the "modern" gospel music. Urcile took the radio home with her every day.

My grandmother was Margaret Eleanor Gibbs Taylor when she was introduced to Hugh Swinton McGillivray. I was two years old when she married him, and I spent most of my summers in their yellow Georgian house by the creek. Mimmie, my great-grandmother, had run a string of boarding houses after her young husband died, leaving her with four young daughters to raise. She taught my grandmother how to cook and keep house for a crowd, making it all seem effortless. People who knew my grandmother Margie before she married Uncle Swinton always mention her cooking, especially her homemade rolls. I remember her being in the kitchen only when she was making her special pink or green mints for holidays, which she'd set on a marble slab out on the back porch across from the ice box.

Urcile did the cooking. We had hominy and liver pudding, hominy and cold fried fish, or hominy and fish roe for breakfast and suppers, fried chicken or fried seafood for dinner at one or two o'clock. There was always rice at dinner—red, when we had seafood, or white, steaming hot with sieva beans, cooler with gravy, or cold in hot vegetable soup.

Dolly Gambrell

Conch Fritters

1 large or two small conchs, cleaned
½ bell pepper
2 small onions
2/3 cup flour
½ tsp. baking powder
1 egg
1 tsp. lime juice
½ tsp. salt

Chop or grind conch, bell pepper, and onion. Add flour, baking powder, unbeaten egg, lime juice, and salt. Mix and drop by spoonfuls into hot fat. Fry until brown.

Bernadette Humphrey

Calamari

Clean squid by pulling the speckled membrane off the outside. Hollow out the body. Inside the head is a hard, sharp portion called the beak. Squeeze this out. Then slice the body into 1/8" circles. Leave the tentacles whole. The squid will be easier to cut up if you partially freeze the clean bodies.

Soak the squid in hot sauce. I use Texas Pete. Coat with a mixture of flour, seafood breader, and a touch of garlic salt.

Deep fry in hot oil until golden brown. Serve with a horseradish sauce or ranch dressing.

Sara Nell Scott

Mikkel Johansen

Dale Rosengarten

Soups and Stews

Drum fish in the spring, sheepshead in the summer, and bass in the fall gave three seasons of sport. Sheepshead are deep-bodied, spiny-finned relatives of porgies, equipped with broad incisor teeth for crushing mollusks. They are outstanding when eaten fresh. Lands End planters constructed feeding grounds for sheepshead by sinking wooden arbors in Broad River, near shore, to which barnacles and oysters could attach. Other favored species of fish taken on hook and line included whiting, blackfish, and cavally. Cavally are narrow-bodied, fork-tailed relatives of pompano, visitors from tropical waters. They were esteemed the tastiest of all game fish.

Theodore Rosengarten, *Tombee: Portrait of a Cotton Planter* (New York: William Morrow, 1986).

Dr. Billy's Shrimp-Corn Chowder

1 quart corn, fresh cut
1 quart new potatoes, washed and cut up
1 small onion, diced
1 quart water
1 tsp. salt
1 quart shrimp
1 quart milk
4-6 oz. sour cream

Combine everything but the shrimp and cook at a low boil until potatoes are done. Peel shrimp. Add to hot ingredients and bring back to a boil for about 8 minutes. Turn off heat. Add milk and sour cream. Keep covered for 30 minutes. Adjust seasoning. Serves 6 to 8.

Billy Dinwiddie

Shrimp-Corn Chowder

1 cup chopped celery
½ cup chopped onion
3 Tbs. butter
1 can cream of mushroom soup
1 can cream-style corn
1 cup milk
1 cup cooked shrimp, chopped
Salt and pepper to taste
Tabasco to taste

In a 3-quart pot, sauté celery and onions in butter until vegetables are clear. Add mushroom soup, cream-style corn, and milk. Add shrimp, salt, pepper, and Tabasco to taste. Heat thoroughly, stirring well. Serve immediately. Serves 4 to 6.

Suzanne Britt

Keith's Shrimp Soup

1 lb. raw shrimp, peeled and deveined
1 small onion
1 Tbs. oil
1 can cream of mushroom soup
1 can water

Sauté onions and shrimp in oil until onions are tender and shrimp are pink. Add soup and water and cook over low heat until good and hot. Serve in a bowl with cooked grits or rice.

Keith Swindell

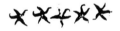

*On the glaring sea
shrimp boats in the haze
the heat*

Sam Savage, *Trawlers*, 1994.

Margie's Shrimp Gumbo

2 lbs. shrimp, cooked and shelled
2 cups hot water
2 cups canned or stewed tomatoes
16 pods okra, sliced
1 small onion, minced
½ cup rice
1½ tsp. salt
3 slices bacon, diced
2 Tbs. flour
Dash of cayenne pepper
1 bay leaf

Cook bacon and onions in frying pan until bacon is crisp and onions are transparent. Remove bacon and onions and add flour; cook 5 minutes, stirring until browned. Put tomatoes, water, okra, and shrimp into soup kettle. Add bacon-onion mixture, bay leaf, and salt and pepper to taste. Add cayenne. Simmer 1 hour. Serve in large soup plates over hot cooked rice.

Margie Leland

Low Fat Sausage and Shrimp Gumbo

1 lb. low fat sausage
2 qts. chicken or shrimp stock (skim the fat, and throw in a
      little Old Bay seasoning)
3 cloves garlic, chopped
3 lbs. shrimp, cleaned and shelled
2 Tbs. Jambalaya seasoning
1 Tbs. gumbo filé
2 cups chopped onion
1½ cups chopped green, yellow, and red bell peppers
1 bag frozen okra, or two cans
2 cups water

Brown the sausage in a large pot; break up into bite-size chunks. Pour off all the grease and let sausage rest on paper towels until ready to use. Add a little chicken broth to the pot along with the garlic, shrimp, and seasonings. Sauté for 3 to 5 minutes. Add the cooked sausage, the onions and peppers, the stock and the okra. Add the water. Simmer for 45 minutes to an hour. To serve, ladle over rice and pass the hot sauce.

Clare Graf

Spicy Seafood Gumbo

3 medium potatoes, peeled and diced
2 medium zucchini, chopped
1 medium sweet onion, chopped
3 to 4 cloves garlic, minced
1 large bell pepper, seeded and chopped
3 Tbs. olive oil
12-oz. package frozen corn
Basil, parsley, white pepper, garlic, and salt to taste
1 2-oz. can tomato paste
4 to 5 shakes of Tabasco sauce
1 8-oz. can spicy V-8
¼ lb. each oysters, clams, and shrimp
      (or substitute any mild fish)

Sauté chopped vegetables in olive oil until tender. Add corn and spices and bring to a boil. Reduce heat and add tomato paste, V-8, Tabasco, and seafood. Stew on low heat for 25 minutes; add tomato paste as needed to thicken. Serve with spicy cornmeal muffins.

Deborahlee Barr

Gigi's Oyster Stew

1 lb. shucked oysters
½ lb. bacon
1 small onion, chopped
½ bell pepper, chopped
½ red pepper, chopped
2 cups half-and-half
1 tsp. Worcestershire sauce
Salt and pepper to taste
Chopped parsley

Cook oysters in their own juice over low heat until edges curl. Drain. Fry bacon. Remove and crumble. Sauté onions and peppers in some of the bacon grease. Combine with cream and seasonings and heat. Do not boil. Serve topped with crumbled bacon, chopped parsley, and oyster crackers.

Bonnie Riedesel

W. Dawsey's Oyster Boat Stew

Fry bacon or fatback until crisp. Remove the meat. Sauté oysters 2 to 3 minutes in a small amount of grease. Add salt and pepper to taste. Serve over rice.

Edith Moses

Miss Helen's Oyster Stew

Heat 4 cups of milk. Add a pint of oysters, 1 Tbs. butter, and salt and pepper to taste. When the oysters curl, the stew is done.

Helen Satterlee

Oliver Banks

Bubba's Oyster Stew

½ lb. smoked jowl or butt meat
3 or 4 medium onions, diced
1 Tbs. vegetable oil
1 quart milk
2 to 4 pints shucked oysters
1 tsp. Nature's Seasons
½ stack saltines

Dice jowl (skinless) into 1/4" to 1/8" cubes—the smaller the better. Substitute bacon if absolutely necessary. Fry in skillet over medium heat until nicely browned. Drain grease and set meat aside. It should be crisp. Sauté onions in 1 Tbs. vegetable oil over medium heat until soft and starting to brown. Set aside.

Heat milk in a medium to large saucepan over medium heat until hot (just starting to steam). Do not boil.

Add to milk while continuing to heat: browned jowl, onions, oysters and their juice, and Nature's Seasons. Heat and stir frequently until oysters crinkle on edges. Crush saltines in hands over pan and drop in. Stir in. Check seasoning and add more Nature's Seasons if necessary.

Robert J. "Bubba" Graham

Easy Oyster Stew

1 quart oysters
1 quart water and oyster liquor
1 stick margarine
1 quart evaporated milk
Black pepper

Cook oysters in water, liquor, and margarine until done. Take off fire and stir in milk and pepper to taste. Serves 4 to 6.

Peggy Livingston

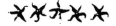

Oysters rattling onto the deck
the scrape of boots
the cold

Sam Savage, *Trawlers*

Lisa's Oyster Stew

½ cup diced celery
½ cup diced onions
¼ cup margarine
1 pint oysters, with juice
Milk
White pepper
Dash of Old Bay seasoning

Sauté celery and onions in margarine. Add oysters and juice, milk, white pepper, and Old Bay. Cook until oysters curl around the edges.

Lisa Mace

Lee Arthur

Pine Bark Fish Stew

10 small flat fish, fresh or saltwater
3 medium onions
5 slices bacon
½ plug [½ stick] butter or oleo
1 bottle tomato catsup
1 can tomato juice

Salt fish, and place a small piece of onion on each. Cut bacon in pieces about 1½" long and fry in a heavy pot. When crisp, take bacon and grease out of pot, put in one layer of fish, sprinkle with finely cut onions and bacon, dot with butter, and pour catsup and tomato juice over all.

Continue making layer after layer in this order until all the fish are used. If necessary, add just enough water so the liquid can be seen. Don't stir while cooking. Let it come to a boil and continue cooking for 25 to 30 minutes on low heat. Keep tightly covered. Serve fish whole with a pancake turner. Add salt and pepper to taste. Some like it hot.

Mrs. R. M. Brailsford, in *McClellanville, S.C. Favorite Recipes,* published by the New Wappetaw Presbyterian Ladies' Aid Society, 1956.

Prevost's Fish Stew

4 slices bacon
4-5 onions, sliced
2 lbs. fish, cleaned, boned, and cut into chunks
2 potatoes, sliced
1 16-oz. can stewed tomatoes with juice
Water
Salt and pepper

Brown bacon and onions in a large pot or stove-top casserole. Add a layer of fish, then potatoes; pour tomatoes and juice over. (I put tomatoes in the blender to break up large pieces.) Add water to cover. Salt and pepper to taste. Simmer until fish is cooked. Serve over rice. This works well in a crock pot too. Serves 4.

Ginny Prevost

Ascan's Catfish Stew

3 lbs. dressed catfish
½ lb. streak-of-lean bacon, sliced and cut in small pieces
3 medium onions, diced
2 large cans stewed tomatoes
5 or 6 medium red potatoes, diced
Salt and pepper to taste

In a very large pot, almost cover the catfish with water and boil until done. Remove bones and reserve liquid. Fry streak-of-lean until brown, then add diced onion and fry until limp. Combine meat, onions, tomatoes, potatoes, and broth in a large pot. Cook until potatoes are almost done. Add catfish and simmer until potatoes are tender and flavors are blended. You may add hot red pepper to taste. If there is not enough broth, add water.

Ascan Sullivan

Shrimp Festival Fish Stew

Every first Saturday in May, you can taste this fish stew along with many other local dishes at the Shrimp Festival and Blessing of the Fleet sponsored by Archibald Rutledge Academy.

1 lb. pork butts meat
4 lbs. onions
4 lbs. potatoes
8-10 lbs. flounder fillets
4 gallon cans crushed tomatoes
Hot sauce, salt, and pepper to taste

Fry butts meat. Remove the meat. Sauté onions in the drippings; add chopped potatoes and all remaining ingredients. Add 4 gallon tomato cans water. Bring to a boil and simmer for about 7 hours. Shut off heat and seal tight overnight. Serves 100.

Mary Scott

New England Codfish Chowder

Our family has always preferred its codfish chowders with milk, never tomatoes, and its snapper, perch, and bass stews with tomatoes, never milk.

8 slices bacon
1 cup chopped potatoes
½ cup chopped onion
¼ cup flour
¼ tsp. salt
4½ cups milk
1 lb. cod

Cook bacon until crisp. Drain, crumble, and set aside. Add potatoes and onion to ¼ cup bacon grease; cook until tender. Stir in flour and salt; blend well. Add milk and diced cod and cook, stirring, until thickened. Do not boil. Garnish with parsley or fennel. Serves 4.

Dolly Gambrell

Dilled Cucumber Soup
with Smoked Salmon Garnish

4 medium cucumbers, peeled, seeded, and chopped
2 shallots or 1 small bunch scallions, peeled and chopped
2 Tbs. lemon juice
½ cup plus 1 Tbs. finely chopped fresh dill
2 cups chicken broth, cold
2 cups low fat yogurt
Salt and finely ground pepper to taste
2 slices Nova Scotia or other smoked salmon, cut into
       small pieces

Puree cucumbers, shallots, lemon juice, and ½ cup dill in food processor with steel blade. Transfer puree to a bowl. Add chicken broth and yogurt, stirring to blend. Season with salt and pepper; chill 3 to 4 hours.

To serve, stir well, ladle into chilled bowls, and garnish with remaining dill and smoked salmon. Serves 4.

Penn Gregg, Millbrook Plantation

Mediterranean Fish Soup

2 large onions, chopped
1 tsp. fennel leaves or chopped fennel bulbs
¼ cup olive oil
4 large ripe tomatoes
2 lbs. fresh fish
Fresh thyme
2 cloves garlic
½ tsp. marigold leaves for color
Lemon verbena
Salt and pepper
Lemon
Garlic croutons (day-old French bread, rubbed with mashed
        roasted garlic, diced, and oven-dried)

Sauté onions and fennel in olive oil over low heat. Turn up
the heat and add tomatoes. Add fish, thyme, and garlic. Stir
well. Add 2 parts cold water to the hot base. Bring to a
boil, then simmer about 20 minutes. Strain; remove garlic,
and press to extract the juice. Discard the solids.

The soup may be cooled and refrigerated at this point,
without salt or pepper. When reheating, add a little lemon
verbena, salt, and pepper. To garnish, sprinkle with lemon
verbena leaves, pot marigolds, or fennel leaves in summer,
lemon wedges or lemon zest in the winter. Serve with
garlic croutons.

Dolly Gambrell

Terry's Clam Chowder

8 strips bacon
1 large yellow onion, diced
¾ lb. potatoes, diced
1½ pints bottled clam juice
2 cups clam liquor
½ tsp. white pepper
1½ pints clams, chopped
10 Tbs. butter
1¼ cups flour
1½ cups milk
6 Tbs. light cream

In a large kettle, brown bacon until crisp. Remove bacon and crumble into small pieces. Remove bacon drippings, strain, and return 2 Tbs. to kettle. Add onions and sauté until translucent. Do not brown.

Add potatoes, clam juices, bacon crumbs, and white pepper.

Turn heat to high and bring to a boil. Cook 10 minutes; add clams and cook an additional 10 minutes or until potatoes are tender. Do not overcook. In a second pot, melt butter over low heat. Stir in flour; cook on low heat and continue stirring about 3 minutes to make a roux. Do not brown. When potatoes are tender, stir the roux into the kettle. Bring back to a boil and remove from heat. In a separate saucepan heat milk and cream. Do not boil or it will curdle. When hot, add to chowder. Serve immediately

or keep in refrigerator overnight. It's even better the second day.

For a lower fat version, substitute 2% or skim milk for the milk and cream. The amount of roux can be cut by half, if half of the potatoes are removed from the kettle when tender and before clams are added. The potatoes are then added to the hot milk and placed in a blender or food processor and pureed until smooth. This mixture is added back to the kettle before the clams. Heat the chowder (do not boil) until clams are tender.

Terry L. Couch

Gabe's Clam Chowder

3 slices salt pork
4 potatoes, cubed
1 quart clams, chopped fine
1 medium onion, chopped

Fry out salt pork until light brown (or use olive oil). Add the other ingredients and 1 quart of water. Cook slowly 1 to 1½ hours, no longer. Serves 6.

Gabe Purvis

Shorty's Clam Chowder

We freeze our clams in the shells, then place them in warm water for a few minutes. Open and chop while frozen, cutting out the black part.

1 large onion, chopped
1 large bell pepper, chopped
3 or 4 carrots, diced small
2 or 3 potatoes, diced small
1 can tomatoes, chopped
1 pint V-8 juice
2 bay leaves
Salt and pepper to taste
At least 1 dozen chowder clams, chopped (You may use
      conch, scallops, or shrimp instead of clams.)

Sauté vegetables in bacon drippings or oil, stirring often until done. Add tomatoes, V-8, and 2 to 3 quarts water, depending on how thick you want the soup. Add bay leaves, salt, and pepper to taste. Cook at least 30 minutes.

Add clams (the more the better) and clam juice. Cook 1½ to 2 hours. You may add instant potato flakes to thicken if desired. Serves 8 to 10.

Leland (Shorty) McClellan

The Captain's Clam Chowder

2 strips bacon
18 to 24 large clams ("chowders")
1 large onion
1 tsp. black pepper
6 medium potatoes, chopped

Open clams. Retain all of the clam juice. Separate clams, then chop. You can use a blender, but be sure not to cut the clams up too fine. Fry the bacon slowly, and just before it is done, add the onions. Sauté for 1 minute. Add the pepper and the clam juice. Bring to a boil. Add potatoes. When potatoes are half-done, add the chopped clams. After the chowder starts to simmer again, allow it to finish cooking. You can put a spoonful of rice in individual bowls before serving.

Bunny Morse

Conch Chowder

2 lbs. conch, chopped fine
1 large onion, chopped
1 large bell pepper, chopped
3 cloves garlic, chopped
4 small potatoes, cubed
2 carrots, sliced
1 can tomatoes
1 46-oz. can tomato juice
1 8-oz. can tomato sauce
3 to 4 bay leaves
Oregano to taste
Salt, pepper, and hot sauce to taste

In a little butter or olive oil, sauté onions, pepper, and garlic with conch until conch turns white. Add potatoes, carrots, tomato base, and spices and cook 8 hours.

Phyllis Martin

Bernadette Humphrey

Conch Stew

Sauté some bacon and chopped onions. Add water and chopped conch, including the conch cheese (the black spots found on the conch's body). Add some diced potatoes and boil until done. Salt and pepper to taste. Serve over rice.

The Crab Pot Restaurant

First you clean the conch; you either beat 'em out of the shell or freeze 'em for two or three days, then you can pull everything out of the shell, clean it, and dice it up or place it in a grinder. You cook till tender with salt, pepper, and onion (or bell pepper or garlic). Then boil down a ham bone and pour off the grease. Make a nice gravy and serve over rice. No tomato—just pure dee conch itself.

Charles Williams

Cajun Seafood Gumbo

Seafood Stock:
Reserved shrimp shells and tails from gumbo
2½ cups water
2 carrots, halved
2 stalks celery with leaves
1 large onion, cut in large chunks
6 whole black peppercorns
1 bay leaf
3 sprigs fresh parsley
3 small cooked crabs, cut in half

Combine all ingredients in a pot and bring to a boil over high heat. Reduce heat and simmer 2 hours. Strain.

Roux:
1/3 cup vegetable oil
1/3 cup all-purpose flour

Combine in a small skillet and cook over medium high heat, stirring constantly, 15 minutes or until the color of peanut butter.

Gumbo:
½ cup vegetable oil
1 large onion, chopped
1 large bell pepper, chopped
3 stalks celery, chopped
6 cloves garlic, minced
1 Tbs. ground red pepper

½ tsp. ground white pepper
½ tsp. dried thyme
½ tsp. filé powder
¼ tsp. ground black pepper
1 bay leaf
1½ quarts seafood stock
2½ lbs. medium-size fresh shrimp
½ lb. fresh crabmeat
½ tsp. salt
1 12-oz. container standard oysters, undrained
½ tsp. salt

Cook onion, bell pepper, and celery in oil in a large pot over medium high heat, stirring often, until tender.

Add garlic and next 5 ingredients; cook, stirring often, until garlic is tender. Add about ¼ cup seafood stock to roux, stirring until blended. Add roux mixture, remaining stock, and bay leaf, stirring until blended. Bring mixture to a boil. Reduce heat and simmer, stirring occasionally, for 1 hour.

Skim fat from surface. Return mixture to a full boil; add shrimp and cook 3 minutes, stirring often.

Add crabmeat; cook 3 minutes, stirring often.

Add oysters; cook 2 minutes, stirring often. Add salt. Remove and discard bay leaf. Serve over rice. Garnish with chopped green onions and fresh parsley if desired. Serves 12.

Gabe Purvis

Anthony Sanders starts a net.

Entrées

In the fall of 1970 I was running the "Sherry Ann" and Baby Ray Jenkins was my striker. There was nothing on the boat but catsup and Pepsi Colas. Baby Ray would bring sea water to a boil, then throw in shrimp with their heads still on. Then he'd bring them to a boil again and pour off all but two cups of the water. He'd stir catsup into this remaining brine and then pour that over the shrimp and stir it around with his hands and serve. We ate it out of the pot. The sauce stuck to your hands while you were heading and peeling the shrimp and then rubbed back onto the shrimp as you put it in your mouth. Towards the end of November there was not even catsup and Pepsi Colas left on the boat. I would take handfuls of the "winter shrimp" (80 count) and throw them on the muffler flange. After about 15 minutes they got crisp and you could eat them head and all. They tasted sweet. One day I found a Pepsi Cola in the bottom of the tool locker. I hid it from Baby Ray and drank it.

William P. Baldwin

Oven-Fried Shrimp with Pecan Coating

1/3 cup all-purpose white flour
¼ cup dark beer
1 large egg white
½ tsp. salt
¾ cup fine, dry, unseasoned bread crumbs
½ cup finely chopped pecans
¼ tsp. freshly ground black pepper
¼ tsp. paprika
1 lb. medium shrimp, peeled and deveined
4 lemon wedges

Preheat oven to 400°. Lightly oil a rack large enough to hold shrimp in a single layer. Put the rack on a baking sheet and set aside.

In a medium-sized bowl, whisk together flour, beer, egg white, and ¼ tsp. salt until creamy and smooth. In a second bowl, stir together the bread crumbs, pecans, pepper, paprika, and remaining ¼ tsp. salt.

Dip shrimp in the breadcrumb/pecan mixture, then the egg mixture, and again in the breadcrumb/pecan mixture. Set the shrimp on the prepared rack so that they do not touch. Bake for 12 to 15 minutes, until golden brown on the outside and opaque in the center. Serve immediately with lemon wedges. Serves 4.

Marsha Purvis

Shrimp Fried in Beer Batter

This is a wonderfully light and fluffy batter that never fails.

1 lb. large shrimp
1 can of beer
1 cup flour, approximately
Oil for deep frying

Peel shrimp, leaving tails on. Combine beer and flour, adding more flour if necessary. Stir until smooth and the consistency of lightly whipped cream, thick enough to hold onto shrimp. Batter should sit at least 10 minutes before using, and may sit up to an hour.

Heat oil to temperature hot enough to brown shrimp in 1 to 2 minutes. Dip shrimp in batter, holding by the tail. Put in hot oil and cook until lightly browned. Drain on paper towels and keep warm in a 200° oven while frying additional shrimp.

Serve with cocktail sauce, honey-mustard sauce, Chinese duck sauce, or sweet and sour sauce for dipping. Serves 4.

Cynthia Kephart

Blackened Shrimp

3 to 4 lbs. shrimp, peeled
¼ cup olive oil
1 Tbs. blackened seasoning (or more, to taste)
2 Tbs. lemon juice

Combine ingredients and marinate shrimp 2 hours or more. Heat a Teflon pan on medium high. Cook shrimp in marinade, stirring constantly, until pink. Serve over spaghetti.

Lisa Mace

Holland Youngman

Low Fat Shrimp Victoria

½ medium onion, diced
4 oz. fresh sliced mushrooms
2 Tbs. low fat margarine
1 lb. shrimp, peeled and deveined
4 oz. light or nonfat sour cream

Sauté onions and mushrooms in margarine. Add shrimp and cook until light pink. Add sour cream and simmer on very low heat for 10 minutes. Serve over rice or pasta. Serves 4.

This recipe was revised to reduce the fat. The original came from a collection of shrimp recipes produced by the South Carolina Shrimpers Association.

Marylou High

Shrimp Nan-G

I've named this dish for a grand Cajun lady who is no longer with us—and I miss her.

½ cup butter
1 medium onion, minced
1 stalk celery, finely chopped
1 carrot, finely chopped
¼ tsp. thyme
2 lbs. large shrimp, in their shells
¼ cup cognac or brandy
1½ cups cream
½ cup milk
1/3 cup sherry
½ cup béchamel sauce (see recipe, p. 221)
½ tsp. salt
1 tsp. lemon juice
¼ cup butter

In a skillet heat ½ cup butter. Add the onion, celery, carrot, and thyme. Cook 10 minutes, or until vegetables are tender and lightly browned. Add the shrimp and cognac. Ignite the cognac and let the flame burn out. Cook for 10 minutes until most of the liquid has evaporated. Stir frequently and be careful that the vegetables do not burn. Remove the shrimp, cool slightly, then remove shells. To the skillet add the cognac, cream, milk, sherry, and béchamel sauce; simmer for 10 minutes, or until the sauce is the consistency of heavy cream. Add the salt and lemon juice. Replace shrimp and heat for 5 minutes. Remove shrimp to a hot

serving dish. Swirl ¼ cup butter into sauce and strain over the shrimp. Serve with rice pilaf. Serves 4 to 6.

Adam Howard

Mrs. Leland's Shrimp Pie

3 slices bread, cubed
1 cup milk
2 cups cooked shrimp
2 Tbs. melted butter
3 eggs, well beaten
1 cup chopped bell pepper and celery, mixed
Salt and pepper to taste

Soak bread in milk and mash with fork. Add shrimp, butter, eggs, vegetables, and seasoning. Turn into buttered casserole and bake in moderately hot oven about 20 minutes. Serves 4 to 6.

Mrs. Rutledge B. Leland, Sr., *McClellanville, S.C. Favorite Recipes,* compiled by the Ladies' Aid Society of the New Wappetaw Presbyterian Church, 1956.

Ladies' Aid Society Shrimp Pie

8 crackers, crumbled
1 quart picked, boiled shrimp [peeled and deveined]
1 stick butter
¾ quart milk [3 cups]
2 Tbs. Worcestershire sauce
1 egg
1 tsp. mustard
Salt and pepper to taste
3 Tbs. catsup
½ Tbs. hot sauce

Put a layer of cracker crumbs in a casserole dish, then a layer of shrimp. Dot with butter. Repeat this until the dish is full. Mix remaining ingredients; pour over shrimp and cracker crumbs. Bake in a hot oven long enough to set well.

Mrs. J. Langley Taylor, Sr., *McClellanville, S.C. Favorite Recipes,* compiled by the Ladies' Aid Society of the New Wappetaw Presbyterian Church, 1956.

Crab and Shrimp Quiche

4 eggs
½ lb. each of cooked shrimp and crabmeat
1 cup finely diced celery
1 cup grated sharp cheese
3 Tbs. sherry
1½ cups mayonnaise
1¼ tsp. Worcestershire sauce

Beat eggs until frothy. Add remaining ingredients and pour into buttered casserole. Bake 1 hour at 325° or until a knife inserted in the middle comes out clean.

Maxine Sullivan

Rafael Rosengarten

Sally Cade

Ted's Popcorn Shrimp

Peel 2 lbs. shrimp.

To make the pastry batter:

Put 6 oz. plain, unbleached flour in a bowl (this is just under 1½ cups). Add ½ tsp. salt and 6 Tbs. olive oil, stirring constantly. Add just enough water to make as thick as cream. Whisk all together.

Separate 2 eggs and beat whites until stiff. (Yolks are not used in this recipe.) Fold egg whites into batter gently, using a rubber spatula.

To fry shrimp:

Heat vegetable shortening in a heavy frying pan for deep-frying. (Fat should be 1" deep.) Dip shrimp in batter and allow excess to drain off. Fry until crisp. Use a spoon or spatula to turn shrimp. Drain on a rack with paper towelling underneath. Serve immediately.

Ted Rosengarten

Boat Shrimp

I call this recipe "boat shrimp" because we used to make them this way when we went fishing at the Cape. It only requires ingredients you keep on your boat. Small creek shrimp are best for flavor.

1 Tbs. butter or margarine
A mess of shrimp (about 2 lbs.)
A piece of Vidalia onion (about ½), cut in very thin slices
Garlic salt, seasoning salt, and basil to taste
2 Tbs. flour
1 Tbs. vinegar

Grab a cast iron pan; set it on the stove. Melt margarine on medium-high heat. Add shrimp and onion; stir while cooking until shrimp are coated. Sprinkle on spices to taste. Sprinkle on flour; turn and coat shrimp. Add enough water to make a gravy. Add vinegar. Serve over rice.

George Stroman, Jr.

Shrimp Curry

2 Tbs. butter
1 small apple, diced
1 small onion, chopped
1 Tbs. curry powder
2 Tbs. flour
1 cup half-and-half
Salt to taste
1½ cups shrimp, shelled and cooked
¼ cup dry sherry
2 cups cooked rice

Melt butter in a frying pan over low heat. Add the apple, onion, and curry powder. Sprinkle with flour, stirring. Add the half-and-half. Add the salt and cooked shrimp. Add sherry last. When thickened, remove from heat and serve over rice. Serves 2.

Blanche Shore, contributed by her daughter, Blanche Oswald

Baked Shrimp–Quick and Easy

1 lb. shrimp, shelled
¼ cup butter
4 cloves garlic, minced
¼ cup white Worcestershire sauce (Lea and Perrins)

Peel shrimp. Melt butter. Add garlic and Worcestershire.
Put shrimp in an 8" baking dish or divide into 4 individual
ramekins. Pour sauce over shrimp. Bake 10 minutes in a
350° oven.

Spoon over rice. Serves 4.

Cynthia Kephart

Olivia Williams

Shrimp-Stuffed Potatoes

6 large potatoes, washed and baked
¾ to 1 lb. raw shrimp, peeled
1 clove garlic, minced
2 spring onions, chopped
1 stick butter
1 pint sour cream
3 strips bacon, cooked crisp (optional)
Salt and pepper
Grated cheese

Cut top off potato. Scoop out insides carefully and save in a bowl. Sauté shrimp, garlic, and onion with 1/3 stick butter until shrimp turn pink. Dump into bowl with reserved potato. Add sour cream, bacon, and seasonings. Mix and stuff into potato shells. Top with your favorite cheese. Put in the oven at 350° until cheese melts.

Sherry Browne, T.W. Graham and Company

Shrimp and Asparagus

1 can cream of asparagus soup
1½ cups heavy cream
1 Tbs. olive oil
1 Tbs. Worcestershire sauce
1 large onion, chopped
1 or 2 cloves garlic, minced
1 stalk celery, finely chopped
2-3 lbs. shrimp, peeled, deveined, tails removed
Salt and pepper

Blend soup and cream in a saucepan and set aside. Mix olive oil, Worcestershire sauce, onion, garlic, and celery; sauté until tender. Add shrimp and sauté until just pink. Heat soup and cream mixture; *do not boil.* Pour over shrimp, add salt and pepper to taste, and cook over very low heat, stirring often until shrimp are done. Serve over rice, pasta, or grits.

Margaret Densmore

Shrimp Alfredo

1 Tbs. butter
1 cup shrimp, cleaned and deveined
½ cup sliced mushrooms
½ cup heavy whipping cream
1 beaten egg yolk
½ cup freshly grated Parmesan cheese
Dash each of salt and pepper

Combine butter, shrimp, and mushrooms in a shallow pan. Cook over medium heat until mushrooms are half done.

Whisk together whipping cream and egg yolk. Pour this mixture into the pan and stir until it begins to thicken. Add Parmesan cheese, salt, and pepper.

Pour over angel hair pasta. Makes 2 small servings or 1 large.

Jeff Coan

Sherried Shrimp and Pasta

1 lb. shrimp, peeled and deveined
1 Tbs. butter
½ pint heavy cream
2 Tbs. sherry

Sauté shrimp in butter until light pink. Add heavy cream and sherry. Stir gently and bring to a simmer for 3 to 4 minutes. Serve over pasta.

Serves 4.

Marylou High

Oliver Banks

Linguine with Shrimp, Artichokes, and Mushrooms

3-4 Tbs. olive oil
2-3 Tbs. butter
1 Vidalia onion, sliced into thin wedges, or 1 bunch spring
     onions, chopped
1 clove garlic, crushed
1 8-oz. package fresh mushrooms, sliced
1 lemon, cut into wedges
Crazy Jane's salt
1 to 1½ lbs. shrimp, peeled and deveined
1½ cans chicken broth
Pillsbury sauce and gravy flour
1 16-oz. package linguine
1 jar marinated artichoke hearts
Freshly grated Parmesan cheese.

In a large skillet heat 2 Tbs. olive oil. Sauté onions and garlic. Remove from pan to a plate. Add to pan 1 Tbs. butter and 1 Tbs. olive oil. Sauté sliced mushrooms. Sprinkle with juice of ¼ lemon, 1 Tbs. olive oil, and 1 tsp. Crazy Jane's salt. Remove to plate with onions.

Add 1 Tbs. butter to pan and sauté shrimp until they are pink. Do not overcook. Sprinkle with juice of ¼ lemon and a bit of Crazy Jane's salt. Remove to plate with vegetables. Add chicken broth to pan and boil, stirring to scrape the pan. While this is boiling, sprinkle flour lightly until sauce thickens to the consistency of heavy cream. Return vegetables and shrimp to the pan with sauce and set aside. Cook linguine in several quarts of boiling salted water. Drain.

Just before serving, cut up 1 jar of drained, marinated artichoke hearts into thin wedges. Mix into shrimp and vegetables. Adjust seasoning. Stir over medium heat until warmed. Remove 1 cup shrimp and vegetables to a bowl. Toss pasta with the vegetables and sauce. Put on a warm serving plate. Add reserved shrimp and vegetables on top. Sprinkle with parsley. Serve with freshly grated Parmesan cheese.

Jenny Hane

Holland Youngman

Bet's Shrimp Scampi

1 cup soft butter
4 shallots, finely chopped
4 garlic cloves, crushed
3 Tbs. A-1 steak sauce
2 Tbs. lemon juice
½ tsp. salt
½ tsp. pepper
1 lb. shrimp

Mix and puree the first 7 ingredients in a blender. Peel shrimp, leaving tails attached. Split shrimp lengthwise and spread open. Top with puree. Place in oiled shallow baking pan or dish and broil until done.

Lyda Graham

Scampi Regina Isabella

1 lb. large shrimp, in shell
Juice of ½ lemon
2 Tbs. olive oil
½ tsp. salt
¼ tsp. pepper
1 cup Hollandaise sauce (see recipe, p. 223)

Peel and devein the shrimp; arrange in a shallow baking dish. Sprinkle with lemon juice, olive oil, salt, and pepper. Broil the shrimp for 3 or 4 minutes, turn and broil 3 or 4 minutes longer. Spoon warm Hollandaise over the shrimp and broil about 2 minutes, or until top is lightly browned. Serves 2 to 4.

Adam Howard

Shrimp and Wild Rice Casserole

½ lb. mushrooms, sliced
½ cup chopped onion
½ medium-size bell pepper, chopped
¼ cup unsalted butter
12 stuffed olives, sliced
1 Tbs. Worcestershire sauce
Dash of hot sauce
1 lb. shrimp, shelled and cooked
2 cups cooked wild rice
2 cups béchamel sauce (see recipe, p. 221)

In a large skillet sauté mushrooms, onion, and bell pepper in butter until tender. Remove from heat. Add olives, Worcestershire, and hot sauce. Add shrimp and toss to coat. Place the wild rice in a buttered casserole. Spread shrimp mixture over the rice and top with the béchamel sauce. Bake at 300° until good and hot. Serves 4 to 6.

Adam Howard

Laurel Hill Shrimp Casserole

1 lb. shrimp, cooked and cleaned
2 cups chopped celery
½ cup water chestnuts, sliced
2 hard-boiled eggs, chopped
2 Tbs. grated onion
¾ cup mayonnaise
2 Tbs. lemon juice
¼ tsp. salt
½ cup grated cheese
1 cup crushed potato chips

Combine first 5 ingredients. Blend in mayonnaise, lemon juice, and salt; stir into shrimp mixture. Put in a buttered casserole. Top with cheese, then potato chips. Bake at 400° for 20 to 25 minutes.

Jackie Morrison

Miss Judy's Shrimp Casserole

1 bell pepper, chopped
1 onion, chopped
½ cup chopped celery
2 cups cooked rice
3 cups boiled shrimp
1 can mushroom soup
1 can milk
1 cup grated cheddar cheese

Sauté vegetables. Mix with rice, cooked shrimp, soup, and milk. Put in a casserole dish. Sprinkle with cheese. Bake at 350° for 30 minutes.

Judith Fortner

Easy Shrimp Casserole

1 cup V-8 juice
2 cups cooked rice
½ cup chopped bell pepper
2 cups cooked shrimp
1 small onion, grated
1½ cups Pepperidge Farm *seasoned* bread crumbs
¾ stick margarine

Mix juice, rice, pepper, shrimp, and onion and place in casserole dish. Top with bread crumbs mixed with melted margarine. Bake at 350° for 25 minutes.

Bobbie Davis

Shrimp and Rice Casserole

½ cup chopped celery
½ cup chopped green onion
½ cup chopped bell pepper
2 Tbs. butter
3 cups cooked rice
1 can cream of mushroom soup
¼ cup dry sherry
1 can cream of shrimp soup
4 drops Tabasco sauce
1 8-oz. can sliced mushrooms, drained
½ cup sliced almonds
3 cups chopped shrimp

Sauté celery, onions, and bell pepper in butter until soft. Mix with all other ingredients. Put in a 3-quart casserole and bake at 350° for 25 to 30 minutes until hot and bubbly. Serves 6.

Suzanne Britt

Cheese and Shrimp Casserole

¼ lb. fresh mushrooms, sliced
2 Tbs. butter
1 lb. fresh cooked shrimp
1½ cups cooked rice
1½ cups grated cheddar cheese
½ cup cream
3 Tbs. catsup
½ Tbs. Worcestershire sauce
½ tsp. salt
Dash pepper

Sauté mushrooms slowly in butter for 10 minutes, or until tender. Mix lightly with shrimp, rice, and cheese. Combine cream, catsup, Worcestershire sauce, and seasonings. Add to shrimp mixture. Pour into casserole, chill overnight if desired. Bake in a moderate oven (350°), for 25 minutes. Serve with broccoli dressed with butter, grated lemon peel, chopped pimiento, and perhaps mushrooms. Serves 4.

Margie Leland

Shrimp and Boat Gravy

6 slices bacon
1 large onion, chopped
2 cups shrimp, peeled and deveined
3 or 4 Tbs. flour
Water
Salt and pepper to taste
Kitchen Bouquet (optional)

Fry bacon until brown and set aside to drain. Sauté onion and shrimp until onion is tender and shrimp are pink. Remove and place with crumbled bacon. Add flour to remaining grease and brown. Add enough water to browned flour to make gravy as thick or thin as you like. Salt and pepper to taste. You can add a few drops of Kitchen Bouquet to darken gravy if you like. Simmer gravy. Spoon onion, shrimp, and bacon over hot grits or rice and serve with the gravy.

Judi Swindell

Fried Shrimp in Brown Tomato Gravy

Vegetable oil for frying
2 lbs. medium shrimp, peeled and deveined
1/2 cup plus 1/3 cup self-rising flour
2 cans "special" tomato sauce (with peppers and
      onions)
¾ cup water
¼ tsp. salt
Dash of pepper

Heat oil. Dip shrimp in self-rising flour. Lightly fry
shrimp. Remove to drain on paper towels. Turn heat to
medium. Add 1/3 cup self-rising flour to pan drippings.
Stir until brown. Add tomato sauce. Add ¾ cup water,
salt, and pepper. Add fried shrimp and simmer in brown
gravy for 20 minutes. Delicious served over rice.

Carole Allen

Stewed Shrimp

*Take your shrimp; salt, pepper, and flour it down, and then
fry it till it browns a little bit. You put some water in it,
then make a gravy with onions, peppers, and different stuff
like that. We normally have it with grits. Matter of fact, all
the fish we used to eat we eat with grits.*

Charles Williams

Shrimp and Grits

½ lb. bacon, fried and crumbled
1 bunch spring onions, chopped
2-3 cloves garlic, chopped
8-10 mushrooms, sliced
1 lb. shrimp, peeled
Cayenne pepper
½ cup grated white cheddar cheese
Nutmeg
Salt
Grits (follow package directions to make 4 servings)

Fry bacon. Remove and crumble. Pour off some of the bacon grease but not all, and sauté onions and garlic. Add sliced mushrooms and shrimp. Cook until pink. Add cayenne pepper and salt to taste. Add crumbled bacon and keep warm. Cook grits according to package directions. Stir in cheese until melted. Add a pinch of nutmeg and salt to taste.

Serve over grits.

Bonnie Riedesel

Shrimp de Jonghe

This dish was very popular years ago, but you don't see it listed any more. That's a shame because it's easy to make.

1 large clove garlic
¾ cup butter, softened to room temperature
1 tsp. salt
Pinch tarragon
Pinch marjoram
1 cup fine bread crumbs
½ cup dry sherry
3 lbs. shrimp, cleaned and cooked
Chopped parsley

Mash garlic until it is almost a paste, then add butter, salt, tarragon, and marjoram. Cream these together until well blended, then add the bread crumbs and dry sherry. Blend well. In a fairly large buttered baking dish place alternate layers of shrimp and breadcrumb mixture, sprinkling parsley over the top of each layer. Bake at 400° for 20 to 25 minutes and serve at once. Serves 6.

Adam Howard

Shrimp Rice

Boil 1 lb. shelled shrimp. Sauté chopped onion, bell pepper, celery, and mushrooms. Add 1 can beef consommé to juice of shrimp to make 2 cups liquid. Steam 2 cups rice with liquid and vegetables. Add shrimp. Salt and pepper to taste.

Sara Graham, contributed by Margie Leland

Boiled Shrimp

To a pot of water add some chopped bell pepper and celery, shrimp boil, salt and pepper, and catsup. Bring to a boil and add fresh shrimp. Boil for 3 minutes and shut off the heat. Allow the pot to cool. Drain and serve.

Ila Mae Cumbee

Potato-Shrimp Salad

3 lbs. shrimp
3 lbs. new potatoes
6 boiled eggs, peeled and diced
Sweet cubed pickles
1 bell pepper, finely chopped
Salt and pepper to taste
Mayonnaise
Paprika

Boil shrimp until they turn pink. Do not overcook. Peel shrimp. Cook potatoes until tender. Mix together shrimp, potatoes, eggs, pickles, bell pepper, salt, pepper, and enough mayonnaise to moisten all ingredients. Garnish with paprika.

Emily Ackerman

Potato Salad With Shrimp and Sugar Snap Peas

½ lb. sugar snap peas
¾ lb. new potatoes
1 lb. shrimp
3 Tbs. chopped shallots
2 Tbs. olive oil
2 Tbs. wine vinegar
¼ cup minced parsley
½ tsp. garlic
¼ tsp. pepper

Cook peas in boiling water 3 to 5 minutes. Boil potatoes and cut in ¼" slices with skins on. Boil shrimp, peel, and devein. Put peas, potatoes, and shrimp in a bowl. Combine remaining ingredients, pour over shrimp, and toss. Serves 4.

Susan Williams

Shrimp and Rice Salad

1 cup raw rice
3 scallions
1 bunch chives
½ onion
1½ cups small cooked shrimp
1 cup mayonnaise
Pinch of ginger
Salt and lemon juice to taste
Lettuce
Sesame seeds, toasted
Paprika

Cook rice and cool. Chop scallions, chives, and onion fine. Add to cold, cooked rice. Add the shrimp and mayonnaise. Season to taste with ginger, salt, and lemon juice and refrigerate until serving time. Heap on lettuce and garnish with sesame seeds and paprika. Serves 5.

Dale Rosengarten

none

Macaroni and Shrimp Salad

1 lb. elbow macaroni
1 cup chopped onion
½ cup chopped celery
½ cup chopped bell pepper
2 lbs. shrimp, cooked, shelled, and deveined
Salt, pepper, celery salt, and paprika to taste
3-4 Tbs. mayonnaise

Cook macaroni as directed on box. Drain and place in a large bowl. Add onions, celery, pepper, shrimp, salt, and spices. Mix with mayonnaise. Chill.

Mae Hutto

 *Entrées*

Miss Minnie Alston's Shrimp Salad

I was born and raised on the Wedge Plantation. My father was the overseer. My grandmother and my mother used to work in the kitchen. I learned to cook from my mother. Being the oldest child, I had to cook for the other eight. I guess I started when I was about ten years old. Biscuits, chicken, potato salad. People in South Santee didn't eat much seafood. I really learned to cook seafood when I got married and moved to Buck Hall.

Steam 1 lb. of shrimp in the shell. To do this, drain it, put it in a pan with a little bacon grease, some chopped bell pepper, chopped onions, seasoned salt, and celery seed. Cook until shrimp is pink—about 5 minutes. Cool the shrimp, peel, remove the sandbags, and chop the shrimp into smaller pieces if they're large.

Meanwhile, hard-boil 6 eggs. Cool, and separate the whites from the yolks. Mash the yolks with 2 Tbs. mayonnaise, a little sweet pickle relish, and a little mustard. This will make a yellow sauce.

Cook 8 oz. of small macaroni shells according to package directions. Rinse in cool water.

Thaw (don't cook) a box of frozen baby sweet peas.

Grate the egg whites. Mix all ingredients together and chill. Serves 4.

Minnie Alston

Michael's Fried Crab

Take the backs off live crabs. (Most people put them in the refrigerator first, to slow them down.) Clean the gills, and wash well. Dredge in flour, salt, and pepper; deep fry for 2 to 3 minutes in vegetable shortening mixed with a little butter. Meat will come out of the shell easily.

Michael Simpson

Pulling a crab pot
hand over hand
the swirling water

Sam Savage, *Trawlers*

Barbecued Crabs

Clean any number of crabs, leaving the meat in the bottom half of the shell.

Brush crabs with barbecue sauce. Put on the grill and cook for 15 minutes or so, brushing at intervals with more sauce. Serve hot and enjoy.

Karen Shuler

Soft Shell Crabs

Soft shell crabs, 2 per person
Fresh thyme, 1 sprig for each crab
Flour
Salt and pepper
Cooking oil
Parsley
Lemon wedges

Rinse, clean, and dry crabs. Tuck a small sprig of thyme under the shell of each. Dredge them in flour, salt, and pepper. Heat oil in skillet very hot, and fry crabs about 5 minutes or until they are crisp and brown. Serve with parsley and lemon wedges.

Ellen Saum

Low Fat Crab Cakes

1 lb. special crabmeat
1 egg white
1 Tbs. lime or lemon juice
2 Tbs. low fat or nonfat mayonnaise
½ cup cracker crumbs
Salt
Fresh ground pepper
Low fat margarine or nonstick cooking spray

Combine the first 7 ingredients. Form into patties and roll in a reserve of cracker crumbs. Sauté on medium heat in low fat margarine (or use a nonstick cooking spray instead).

Serves 6 people, 2 crab cakes each.

Marylou High

McClellanville Crab Cakes

1 lb. claw crabmeat
2 eggs, beaten well
1 large onion, diced
2 Tbs. self-rising flour
1 package Sauers Crab Classic
½ tsp. salt
½ tsp. pepper
Vegetable oil

Combine first 7 ingredients; mix well. Form into balls, then flatten into patties. Fry in hot oil until golden brown. After the cakes are cooked, lay them on paper towels to drain excess oil.

Carole Allen

Carolina Crab Cakes

2 slices bread
1 egg, beaten
1 Tbs. mayonnaise
1 tsp. celery salt
1/8 tsp. red pepper
Dash of black pepper
2 Tbs. parsley flakes
¼ tsp. dry mustard
1 Tbs. Worcestershire sauce
1 Tbs. baking powder
1 lb. crabmeat

Crumble bread into small pieces and mix with beaten egg. Add all other ingredients and mix well. Shape into cakes. Fry in hot oil at 375° for about 4 minutes, or until golden brown.

Judith Fortner

Maryland-Style Crab Cakes

2 Tbs. butter
¼ cup minced celery
¼ cup minced onion
1 clove garlic, minced
1 lb. crabmeat, cooked
2 eggs, slightly beaten
½ cup unseasoned bread crumbs
1 Tbs. Worcestershire sauce
1-2 Tbs. Old Bay seasoning

Lightly sauté the celery, onion, and garlic in butter, about 2 to 3 minutes. Combine the crabmeat, eggs, and all other ingredients in a bowl. If mixture is too liquid, add more bread crumbs. Form into 4 patties and dip in bread crumbs. Place in a pan sprayed with a small amount of oil to prevent sticking. Bake in a 400° oven about 25 minutes, turning patties once. Serves 4.

Cynthia Kephart

Deviled Crab or Crab Cakes

6 slices bacon
1 large onion, chopped
1 stalk celery, chopped
½ bell pepper, chopped
1 lb. crabmeat
1 roll Ritz crackers, crushed
1 Tbs. mustard
¼ cup mayonnaise
2 tbs. Worcestershire sauce
Tabasco to taste
Paprika
Butter

Fry bacon until crisp and set aside. Sauté onion, celery, and bell pepper until tender. In a bowl, combine the next 6 ingredients. Add onions, celery, bell pepper, and crumbled bacon. Put in a casserole dish. Garnish with paprika and dot with butter. Bake at 400° for 10 to 15 minutes, *or* shape into patties and roll in cracker crumbs and fry in a small amount of oil until brown.

Judi Swindell

Deviled Crab

3 Tbs. butter
2/3 cup chopped celery
½ cup chopped bell pepper
4 cups crabmeat, cooked
1 cup cracker crumbs
2 Tbs. mayonnaise
2 Tbs. prepared mustard
2 Tbs. Worcestershire sauce
¼ tsp. salt
½ tsp. black pepper
2 eggs

Place butter, celery, and pepper in a small amount of water. Cook until tender. Add remaining ingredients. Mix all together. Place in a casserole which has been well greased. Dot top with butter. Bake at 350° for 10 to 15 minutes.

Ruth J. Morrison, submitted by Nickie Ellis

McClellanville Bed and Breakfast Deviled Crab

3 Tbs. butter or margarine
1 medium bell pepper, chopped fine
1 small onion, chopped fine
½ cup chopped celery
1 lb. crab meat (I use part white and part claw)
2/3 cup cracker crumbs (Ritz are good)
2 heaping Tbs. mayonnaise
½ tsp. Worcestershire sauce
1 tsp. mustard
Salt and pepper
1 egg

Sauté the vegetables in butter or margarine until tender. Cool. Mix in remaining ingredients. If mixture is too dry, add another egg or more mayonnaise. If it is too damp, add more cracker crumbs. Place in shells or a casserole, well buttered. Bake at 350° for about 20 minutes.

Shirley McClellan

Dolly's Deviled Crab

¼ cup butter
¼ bell pepper, chopped
¼ cup all-purpose flour
¼ tsp. salt
White pepper and allspice to taste
1 tsp. Dijon mustard
2 cups milk
1 Tbs. lemon juice
¼ cup dry white wine or milk
2 eggs
½ cup mayonnaise
1 cup cooked rice
1 lb. cooked crabmeat
1 Tbs. chopped parsley

Crumb topping:
¼ cup butter
¾ cup soft bread crumbs
¼ cup Parmesan cheese

Prepare crumb topping by mixing all ingredients. In a large frying pan over medium heat, melt butter. Add pepper and cook for about 5 minutes. Blend in flour, salt, pepper, allspice, and mustard; cook, stirring, until sauce thickens. Remove from heat; add lemon juice, wine, eggs, mayonnaise, rice, crab, and parsley. Mix well. Spread in a shallow 2-quart baking pan or 6 ramekins. Sprinkle with crumb topping. Bake, uncovered, in a 350° oven until

browned and bubbly, about 30 minutes for a casserole, 20 minutes for ramekins.

Dolly Gambrell

Crab

3 Tbs. butter
2/3 cup chopped celery
½ cup chopped bell pepper
½ cup chopped onion
4 cups crabmeat
1 cup cracker crumbs
2 Tbs. mayonnaise
2 Tbs. prepared mustard
2 Tbs. Worcestershire sauce
¼ tsp. salt
½ tsp. black pepper
2 eggs

Boil the butter, celery, bell pepper, and onion in a small amount of water. Add remaining ingredients. Bake in a casserole dish, topped with butter, about 15 minutes.

Found written by hand in Louise Leland Stroman's copy of *McClellanville, S.C. Favorite Recipes,* compiled by the Ladies' Aid Society of the New Wappetaw Presbyterian Church, 1956.

Devilish Crab

½ cup butter
6 Tbs. flour
2 cups hot milk
4 hard-boiled eggs, chopped
2 Tbs. Dijon mustard
1 tsp. dry mustard
1 Tbs. Worcestershire sauce
4 Tbs. finely chopped parsley
2 Tbs. finely chopped onion
2 Tbs. finely chopped bell pepper
1 lb. crabmeat
Cayenne pepper
Salt and freshly ground black pepper
6 Tbs. grated Parmesan cheese

Melt butter in the top of a double boiler; add flour and cook over boiling water, stirring continuously until well blended. Add hot milk slowly, stirring continuously until sauce begins to thicken. (¼ cup dry sherry may be added, cutting milk to 1¾ cups.) Stir in chopped eggs, mustards, Worcestershire, parsley, onion, and bell pepper. Simmer sauce, stirring from time to time, until thick. Flake crab meat and add to sauce, stirring gently so as not to break the meat. Season to taste with cayenne, salt, and ground pepper and fill crab shells or individual ramekins with mixture. Sprinkle top with Parmesan cheese and bake in a 450° oven for 20 minutes. Serves 6.

Adam Howard

Crabmeat Soufflé

2 cups crabmeat, claw or white
1 Tbs. Worcestershire sauce
1 Tbs. French's mustard
2 Tbs. butter
2 Tbs. flour
¾ tsp. salt
1/8 tsp. pepper
1 cup evaporated milk, diluted with 1 cup water
½ cup soft bread crumbs
3 egg yolks
3 egg whites

Season crabmeat with Worcestershire sauce and mustard. Heat butter, add flour, salt, and pepper. Mix well, add milk gradually and bring to a boil, stirring constantly. Add crumbs and cook 2 minutes. Take from fire and add crabmeat and well-beaten egg yolks. Fold in stiffly beaten egg whites. Bake in a greased baking dish at 350° for 50 minutes. The soufflé mixture may be made early; place in refrigerator and add egg whites just before baking. Salmon may be used in place of crabmeat.

Lolita Kelly, from the *McClellanville United Methodist Women's Cookbook*, 1972.

Crab and Artichoke Casserole

1 stick butter
3 Tbs. minced onion
½ cup flour
1 quart cream, heated to boiling
½ cup Madeira wine
Salt and pepper to taste
2 Tbs. lemon juice
4 cups mixed crabmeat and shrimp
3 9-oz. packages frozen or canned artichokes, quartered
2½ cups cooked shell macaroni
2 cups grated Gruyère or Swiss cheese

Melt butter to sizzling. Sauté onions until golden, then stir in flour until mixture is pale yellow. Remove from heat, add cream and stir vigorously. Return to medium heat and bring to a boil. Reduce heat and add wine, salt, and pepper. Pour lemon juice over crab and shrimp and toss with artichokes, macaroni, and sauce. Place in a 6-quart buttered casserole and sprinkle with cheese. Bake 25 to 30 minutes at 350°. Serves 10 to 12 people.

Phyllis Martin

Bet's Crab

1 lb. crabmeat (2 cups)
12 saltines, crushed
Butter the size of an egg
1 Tbs. mayonnaise
2 or 3 eggs, beaten
1 cup milk
1 can evaporated milk
1 tsp. Worcestershire sauce
Salt, pepper, and a dash of nutmeg
2 Tbs. sherry
Dash of mustard

Mix together all ingredients, reserving ½ cup saltine crumbs. Put in a 10" casserole and sprinkle some saltine crumbs on top. Bake at 350° approximately 25 minutes.

Lyda Graham

Mae's Crab Casserole

3 Tbs. butter
2/3 cup chopped celery
½ cup chopped bell pepper
1 cup chopped onion
3 Tbs. mayonnaise
3 Tbs. mustard
3 Tbs. Worcestershire sauce
5 cups crabmeat (stone crab is best)
2 cups Ritz crackers, crushed
2 eggs, well beaten
Salt and pepper to taste
Margarine
Paprika

Mix together first 11 ingredients, reserving ½ cup cracker crumbs. Put in an 8" casserole; top with reserved crumbs, dot with margarine and sprinkle with paprika. Bake at 350° until crackers are brown. (You can also add ½ cup of cooked, shelled, and deveined shrimp.)

Mae Hutto

Ultimate Oyster Pie

Pastry for one pie crust
1 Tbs. minced smoked salmon
2 pints oysters
1 cup half-and-half
2 thin onion slices
1 small bay leaf
Pinch each of celery salt and thyme
1 whole clove
4 eggs
3 Tbs. sherry wine
½ cup grated Gruyère or Swiss cheese, divided
1½ Tbs. butter

Roll out pastry; fit into a 9" pie plate and flute edges. Prick sides and bottom with a fork. Bake at 400° for 10 minutes; remove and cool. Sprinkle with minced salmon.

Drain the oysters, reserving ½ cup liquor. Place half the oysters in the pie crust. Pour cream into a saucepan with onion, bay leaf, celery salt, thyme, and clove. Scald and remove from heat. Add oyster liquor, strain and cool. Beat in eggs, one at a time, without stopping; stir in sherry. Pour half the sauce into the crust, sprinkle with ¼ cup of the cheese and top with remaining oysters. Add the rest of the sauce and top with cheese. Dot with butter. Bake at 350° for 30 minutes or until top is delicately brown. Serves 6 to 8.

Adam Howard

Scalloped Oysters

½ cup Pepperidge Farm stuffing mix
1 quart oysters in their juice
Salt and pepper
1 stick butter
Saltine crackers
1 pint milk
1 pint half-and-half

Spray a 2-quart casserole dish with non-stick cooking oil. Spread ½ cup stuffing mix over bottom. Put a layer of oysters and juice over stuffing. Sprinkle with salt and pepper and dot with butter. Top with a layer of saltines. Add milk just to cover. Repeat, finishing with saltines on top. Dot with butter. Pour half-and-half on top. Bake at 350° for 25 minutes or until liquid has been absorbed and oysters are curled. Serve immediately. Serves 6 to 8.

Suzanne Britt

[The Indians] have a remarkable way of fishing in their rivers. As they have neither steel nor iron, they fasten the sharp, hollow tail of a certain fish (something like a sea crab) to reeds or to the end of a long rod, and with this point they spear fish both by day and by night. Sometimes they also use the prickles and pricks of other fish. And they make traps with reeds or sticks set in the water and narrowing at the ends, as shown in the picture. They have different kinds of fish, many of them never found in our waters, and all of an excellent taste.

Thomas Hariot, *A Brief and True Report of the New Found Land of Virginia*, 1588.

Indian fishing techniques. Engraving by Theodore de Bry after a drawing by John White, c. 1585.

Entrées

Flounder–The Best Way

This is the optimal way to enjoy small flounder, such as the shrimp boats catch, when they are too tiny to fillet.

Fresh flounder, one per person
Italian dressing, or other marinade of your choice
Paprika

Do not scale or gut the flounder but use a very sharp knife to make shallow incisions through the skin on both sides, beginning just behind the head and moving obliquely downward behind the abdominal cavity. At the top and bottom of each incision make small nicks under the skin to allow the corners to be picked up. Use a fish skinner to pull the skin downward toward the tail, shifting from corner to corner to make sure the skin comes off cleanly. Repeat the procedure for the second side.

Remove the head and abdomen by using a heavy knife to deepen the incision line and sever the spinal cord. Wash the fish, removing bloody kidney material from the abdominal cavity.

Marinate the fish in Italian dressing in a zip-lock plastic bag for 30 minutes or longer.

Transfer the fish to a broiling pan, and place the pan in a 350° oven with the uppermost rack close to the heat source. Let the underside of the fish (the thinner side) be on top first. Sprinkle the fish with a little paprika. Bake for about

2 minutes, then turn on the broiler. Broil for 3 minutes, until it looks done. Turn the fish over, sprinkle the thicker side with paprika, then broil it for about 3 minutes. Remove and serve the fish with a spatula. Usually, the fins will be lightly stuck to the pan. Let them fall away or tease them away with the spatula.

This is a fine way to do 2, 3, or 4 fish, and you can double the number if you start baking the second turn while you broil the first ones.

Do not be inhibited by the thought of skinning the fish. It's as easy as scaling or filleting and the end product is most attractive. You can, of course, cook fillets this way. And if you can't bear to skin the fish you can scale it, remove the head and abdomen, and score it on top and bottom before broiling it as described above.

Dr. Walter Bonner

Stuffed Flounder

1 4 to 5 lb. flounder
2 lemons
1 lb. shrimp, chopped
1 lb. clams, chopped
1 lb. crabmeat
2 eggs
2/3 cup chopped onion
1 small loaf cornbread, crumbled
1 Tbs. pepper
3 strips bacon
½ cup fresh dill or lemon verbena

Make a cut down the middle of the flounder from the tail up, then make a fillet cut on each side, leaving the meat in place. Salt fish inside and out. Squeeze lemon juice over fish inside and out.

Put shrimp, clams, and crabmeat in a large bowl. Add eggs, onion, cornbread, and pepper. Mix this up well.

Open the flounder up where cuts were made and stuff with mixed ingredients. Arrange the bacon on top of the fish. Sprinkle with black pepper. Garnish with fresh dill or lemon verbena. Cover with foil. Bake at 375° for 35 to 40 minutes. Serves 8.

Bunny Morse

Blackened Flounder, Catfish, or Tuna

2 flounder, catfish, or tuna fillets
2 Tbs. oil
1 tsp. salt
Cajun blackened fish seasoning

Rub the fillets with oil. Sprinkle with salt. Rub both sides rather heavily with Cajun blackened fish seasoning. Spray a heavy frying pan with nonstick cooking spray. Add 2 Tbs. oil. Heat, add fish, and cook 3 to 5 minutes on each side. If you cook this dish in the kitchen, open the doors and windows, and don't be surprised if your smoke alarm sounds off! The fish may also be grilled outside.

Suzanne Britt

Carlin Rosengarten

Ziggy's Blackened Tuna

4-6 tuna steaks
1 tsp. paprika
1 tsp. salt
1 tsp. onion powder
1 tsp. garlic powder
1 tsp. cayenne pepper
¾ tsp. black pepper
¾ tsp. white pepper
½ tsp. dried thyme
½ tsp. dried oregano
Butter

Mix all dry ingredients well and rub on tuna steaks. Heat a cast iron pan until very hot. Melt butter and add the tuna. For ½"-thick steaks, blacken 2 minutes per side. For ¾" steaks, blacken 3 minutes per side. You can cut a piece to check for doneness. It is better to undercook than to overcook, as the fish will continue to steam when removed from the heat.

Richard Ziegler

Fish and Grits

Breading mix
Salt and pepper
Milk
Whiting or other fish fillets
White grits, cooked
Fresh tomato wedges

Mix salt and pepper with breading mix. Add enough milk to make a batter. Coat fish with butter and deep fry until golden brown. Drain and serve with hot grits and tomato wedges.

Alma Gaskins
Hathaway's Cafe

Annie Banks

Charcoal Grilled Fish

Lightly salt and pepper fish fillets. Place in a grilling basket. Put a little butter on the fish, then a layer of onion, then a layer of bacon strips. Grill on each side until done. Cooking time will depend on the thickness of the fish and the heat of the coals. The meat will flake when done.

Fred Sullivan

Seewee Shad Roe

Wash and drain the roe. Dip into a mixture of eggs and milk, then into cracker meal mixed with a little flour, seasoned with salt and pepper. Fry in hot peanut oil until golden brown. Don't overcook.

Mary Ellen Rancourt
Seewee Restaurant

Boneless Shad

Preheat oven to 300°. Place a 2-3 lb. shad on rack in baking pan. Add to pan:

    4 cups water
    1 cup white wine
    2 stalks celery, chopped
    1 medium onion, chopped
    2 bay leaves

Cover tightly and cook 6 hours.

Phyllis Martin

Will Bigelow

Ginger-Lime Fish Steaks

In a food processor, blend ½ cup butter or margarine with chopped ginger root (a 3" x 1½" piece) until smooth. Place fish steaks in a baking dish. Spread each steak with butter mixture; lay lime slices on top. Cover with plastic wrap. Vent. Microwave on high power 5½ to 6½ minutes or until center begins to flake. Let stand 5 minutes, covered. Serve with any leftover butter mixture and lime wedges.

Ruth Edwards

*In the evening sun
the shadow of a mast
reaches the shore*

Sam Savage, *Eighteen Kinds of Loneliness,* 1995.

Easy Fish Steaks

4 5-oz. fish steaks, about 1" thick

Coat steaks with mayonnaise. Add a bit of dill and cover with plastic wrap. Vent. Microwave on high for 5½ to 6½ minutes or until center of fish flakes. Rotate dish once during cooking. Let stand 5 minutes, covered.

Ruth Edwards

Baked Spot Tail Bass

Flounder or sheepshead may also be used.

Fillet fish. Coat one side of a large piece of aluminum foil with vegetable oil. Salt and pepper fish on both sides. Place on oiled aluminum foil. Sprinkle with oregano. Add several pats of butter. Squeeze some lemon juice over fish. Garnish with sliced potatoes and onions. Fold aluminum foil and wrap tightly around fish and vegetables. Bake at 350° for 40 minutes.

Fried Fish

Sprinkle salt lightly over fish and let stand for at least 30 minutes. Cut fish into pieces, around 3 to 4" wide, and coat with "House of Autry Seafood Breader."

In a small thin pot, heat approximately 4" of vegetable oil. The thin pot helps the oil to reheat quickly when fish is added. Test oil with dab of the breader to see if it's hot enough. Drop coated fish into heated oil a few at a time and cook until brown, 3 to 4 minutes. Drain on paper towels. Shrimp and oysters can be done the same way.

Shirley McClellan

The Vasco da Gama, one of the first Portuguese shrimp boats to come to McClellanville in the 1930s. Richard Lofton painted this watercolor in 1935 for his sister Margaret in exchange for a chocolate cake. Courtesy of Edith Moses.

Rafe's Fried Grouper

1 lb. fillets of grouper, or other firm fish
1 cup milk
1 small onion, minced
1 clove garlic, minced
2/3 cup flour
1/3 cup cornmeal
½ tsp. basil
½ tsp. oregano
1/8 tsp. cayenne
Dash of salt
Black pepper to taste
Light oil for frying

Marinate grouper fillets in mixture of milk, onion, and garlic for 30 minutes. Combine flour, cornmeal, spices, salt, and pepper. Dredge fillets in dry mixture. Heat ½" oil in a heavy pan. Fry fillets in hot oil about 5 minutes per side, or until golden brown.

Serve with lemon wedges or favorite dipping sauce.

This recipe makes a thin, greaseless crust. The key is to use fresh fish. You can vary the recipe by substituting fresh lemon juice for the milk and onion. Keep the garlic.

Rafael Rosengarten

Lee Arthur

Fish Baskets

There was a colored fellow there at Wilcox County sentenced up from Brantley, Alabama. He was a nice talkin young fellow—heavy, chunky-built—he looked about twenty-two or twenty-three years old. Called this colored boy Shakey. He liked me and he loved to talk with me—called me Uncle Nate. And he got to talkin with me one day about makin baskets and what sort of trades did I know. I told him, "I makes baskets and I runs a blacksmith shop and there's a few other things I know how to do, but basketmakin is a special labor with me. I can make any kind of basket, most you want to see—fish basket, feed basket, clothes basket, market basket, cotton basket, any sort of basket in reason."

He said, "Uncle Nate, is that the truth you tellin me?"

I said, "Yes, I can make em."

He went right on and didn't stop until he told Captain Springer, man that worked over us, told him about it. That was a pretty nice white man; he was a Springer, out of Montgomery. He was spare-built, small, and when he walked he sort of toted his head sideways. He come to me, said, "Nate, can you make baskets like I been hearin bout you?"

Told him, "Yes sir, Captain, make you any kind of basket you want."

"Make fish baskets?"

"Yes sir, I make fish baskets; been makin fish baskets off and on every year, all my life, after I got big enough to work white oak."

He said, "Nate, if you makes fish baskets, I want you to make me one. But don't let this old warden here know you makin it for me. He's hell." Old man Frank Castle, he was a cat, too; made them boss men jump—"I'll tell you how to do it"—I was a water boy then, mainly—"I'll put another fellow on your job till you make me a fish basket. You just go out"—the whole state premises was wired up there—"just anywhere on the inside of this wire you can find some white oak, cut yourself what you need and make me a fish basket. You know that great big old pine log down there on the side of the road where you go out the big gate to the public road?"

I said, "Yes sir, I've seen that old pine log there."

Old pine log was seven feet high, what was left of that tree. You could sit down behind it, couldn't nobody see you.

He said, "You get your white oak and sit down there; split it out, do like you want to do it and make me a fish basket. If you'll do that I'll give you all the fish you can eat." Them was his words. And said, "You stay down there. I'll come down there to you once or twice and see how you doin. How long will it take you to make it?"

I said, "O, I can make it in a couple of days."

It would take a couple of days if I wanted it to, or I could do it in one day. But let him put another fellow to totin water and I'll see how I feel settin off and workin white oak. I'd just be off—but I sure stayed where he sent me, I didn't ramble. When they gived me a break thataway or anything happen in my favor, then I'd be submissive—behave and go by orders that's profitable to me. And not let em know I'm enjoyin myself too much.

Might order me that way again. They liked to give orders, a heap of times not for nothin but the givin of em.

So I said, "I know where's some white oak right now. I seed it the other day, over there at the mule lot."

He said, "Well, you go on to where it's at and cut yourself some and make me a fish basket. I'll give you all the fish you can eat."

I went right on off that mornin—mule lot was about a half a mile from the camp—took me a ax and went on. Cut that white oak down, took it on my shoulder and went on down into the swamp until I got to that big pine log. I stayed there two days fooling with that white oak and I made Captain Springer a fish basket about as wide around as my waist or a little wider. I don't do this, usually, but it's easier if it's done: cut a hole in the side of the basket and fix a way to have a little door. He wanted me to put a door to it. My baskets would always catch fish but I never preferred havin a door to empty em. But Lord, I've caught them baskets full of fish up to the muzzle, many a time. I'm a fisherman."

Theodore Rosengarten, *All God's Dangers: The Life of Nate Shaw* (New York: Alfred A. Knopf, 1974).

Oriental Fish

1 Tbs. cornstarch
4 tsp. soy sauce
¾ cup chicken broth
1 Tbs. oil
1 Tbs. minced garlic
1 Tbs. minced ginger
1½ Tbs. vinegar
1 tsp. sugar
Pepper to taste
2 6-oz. fish fillets
Chopped chives

Combine cornstarch and soy sauce in a small bowl. Stir to dissolve cornstarch. Blend into chicken broth. Heat oil in a heavy frying pan over medium heat. Add garlic and ginger; stir-fry about 30 seconds. Add vinegar, broth mixture, and sugar. Stir until sauce thickens, about 12 minutes. Remove from heat; season with pepper to taste. Preheat broiler. Brush some sauce over both sides of the fillets and in bottom of broiling pan. Broil about 3 minutes per side until fish is cooked. Place fillets on plates. Sprinkle with chives. Serve with red rice and pass the remainder of the sauce. Serves 2.

Ginny Prevost

Cheesy Fish

1 lb. fish fillets
¼ tsp. seasoned salt
2 Tbs. butter
1/3 cup sour cream
3 oz. mozzarella cheese, shredded
1 Tbs. chopped parsley

Wipe fish dry and place in an ovenproof dish. Sprinkle with salt and dot with butter. Cover and microwave on high for 2 minutes. Meanwhile, mix sour cream and cheese. Remove fish and spread with sour cream/cheese mixture; sprinkle with parsley. Cover and microwave on high 2 to 3 minutes or until fish is cooked. Serves 2 to 3.

Ginny Prevost

How the Indians Cooked Their Fish

Indians broiling fish over an open fire. Engraving by Theodore de Bry after a drawing by John White, c. 1585.

When the natives have caught enough fish, they assemble in a place where they can easily prepare them. They stick four stakes of equal height into the ground with a number of posts across them. The fish are laid upon the platform, and a fire is built beneath it. After the platform is full of fish and will hold no more, the rest of the catch is hung at the sides, or on sticks close to the fire, until there is room for them. So they cook their whole catch at once, taking good care not to burn the fish. As soon as some are cooked, they are replaced by others; in this way they continue to cook their game until they think they have enough.

Thomas Hariot, *A Brief and True Report of the New Found Land of Virginia*, 1588.

How the McClellanville Methodist Men Smoke Their Mullet

Cut off the heads. Split the fish open down the ribs to the back bone from the underside, but do not cut them in half. Remove the entrails, but *do not scale*. The scales serve as insulation so that the fish will smoke instead of broiling. Make up a salt brine using 1 cup of salt to every gallon of ice water. Soak the fish in the brine for 2 to 3 hours, either in the refrigerator or in a cooler. Drain on a wire rack. Using seasoned hickory or charcoal with hickory chips, make a slow fire in the bottom of a smoker so that the temperature hovers around 115°. Spread out the coals. Place fish in the smoker with scale sides down. Smoke fish 6 to 8 hours over coals covered with water-soaked hickory chips. Add wood or charcoal as needed, and make sure to keep the smoke going. When the fish are golden brown on top, they are done. Smoked mullet will keep for 10 to 14 days in the refrigerator, and may also be frozen.

Bernadette Humphrey

Baked Grouper

½ cup white wine
2 Tbs. lemon juice
1 clove garlic, minced
½ tsp. dill
½ tsp. rosemary
1 tsp. Italian seasoning
½ tsp. pepper
2 lbs. grouper
1 sweet onion, thinly sliced
1 large tomato, sliced
¾ cup low fat Swiss cheese

Mix wine, lemon juice, and spices. Put 2 Tbs. of mixture in a shallow casserole dish and swirl around until the surface is coated. Layer grouper, onion, sauce, and tomato in casserole. Bake at 350° for 20 minutes or until done. Sprinkle with cheese and bake 5 more minutes.

Margie Leland

Roast Tuna

3 slices tuna, 1" thick (about 3 lbs.)
½ cup minced onion
½ cup chopped green onions
½ cup red wine vinegar
¼ cup lemon juice
½ cup melted butter
2 bay leaves
1 tsp. salt
¼ tsp. pepper
1 Tbs. capers

Skin and bone tuna. Wash and drain well on paper towels. Place on rack in roasting pan. Mix onion, green onions, vinegar, lemon juice, butter, bay leaves, salt, and pepper. Pour over tuna. Roast in a hot oven (400°) about 16 minutes, basting often. Place tuna slices on a platter, add capers to sauce, and pour over tuna. Serves 6.

Hugh Kremer

Today, no fishing–
dawn wind
rattling the palmettos

Sam Savage, *Trawlers*

163

Porgy

24 oysters
12 medium clams
1½ cups red wine
6 Tbs. butter
2 onions, sliced
1 4-lb. porgy, cleaned

Bouquet garni:
2 sprigs fresh thyme, or ¼ tsp. dried
1 bay leaf
2 sprigs parsley

Kneaded butter:
2 Tbs. butter kneaded with 2 Tbs. flour

Pinch cayenne pepper
Salt and freshly ground black pepper

Place the oysters and clams with ¼ cup of the wine in a tightly covered pot over high heat and steam for a few minutes until all the shells open. Pour them into a colander placed over a bowl. Remove oysters and clams from their shells, allowing any liquid to drain into the bowl. Keep them barely warm in another bowl, covered. Strain the liquid through several layers of cheesecloth.

In a frying pan over medium heat, cook the onions in 3 Tbs. butter until soft. Spread onions out in the bottom of a large baking dish. Place the fish on top, season lightly with salt

and pepper, add the remaining wine, the shellfish liquid, and the bouquet garni.

Cover the dish with aluminum foil and bake at 350° for about 20 minutes. Transfer the fish to a hot serving platter and keep warm. Reduce the cooking liquid in a saucepan over high heat to about 1½ cups and discard the bouquet garni. Blend in the kneaded butter. (Flour mixed with butter will blend evenly into hot sauce as the butter melts, avoiding small lumps.) Reduce the heat and simmer for about 8 minutes, stirring now and then. Add cayenne and correct the seasoning. Remove from the heat and swirl in the remaining butter, bit by bit. Arrange the oysters and clams around the fish. Pour the sauce over all. Place in a 400° oven for 2 or 3 minutes. Serve at once. Serves 6.

Adam Howard

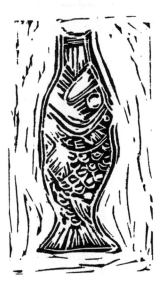

Regana Sisson

165

Foil-Baked Fish

1 Tbs. soy sauce
1 tsp. olive oil
4 fish fillets
4 green onions, thinly sliced
½ cup diced bell pepper
¼ cup diced cucumber
1 Tbs. minced ginger

In a cup, mix the soy sauce and oil. Set aside. Cut squares of foil large enough to fold over the fish and seal, and place 1 fillet in the middle of each. Sprinkle with sliced onions, bell peppers, and ginger. Drizzle each fillet with 1 tsp. soy mixture. Fold foil over fillets and seal tightly. Bake in a 450° oven for 10 to 15 minutes, or until fish is cooked. Serves 4.

Ginny Prevost

Fish Dijon

2 fish fillets
6 Tbs. soft margarine
4 tsp. Dijon mustard
1 tsp. chopped parsley
Salt and pepper to taste
Dry bread crumbs

Place fish on foil in oven-proof dish. Mix the margarine, mustard, parsley, salt, and pepper together and cover each fillet to the edges. Sprinkle with bread crumbs. Bake in a 450° oven for 10 minutes. Serves 2.

Ginny Prevost

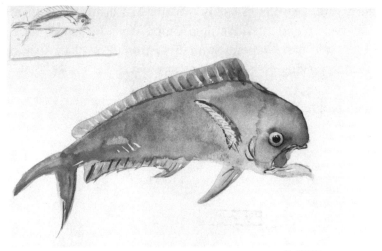

S. Williams

Swordfish with Olive Sauce

2 swordfish steaks, about 1½" thick
2 Tbs. butter
2 Tbs. vegetable oil
¼ cup flour
½ cup chopped onion
1 8-oz. can tomato sauce
1 can or bottle of beer
½ cup chopped stuffed olives
1 tsp. salt
Dash of pepper

Dot swordfish steaks with half the butter; place on a greased broiler rack 3" from heat. Broil about 4 minutes; turn and dot with remaining butter. Broil 4 or 5 minutes more, until fish flakes easily. While fish broils, heat oil in saucepan; blend in flour; add onion, tomato sauce, beer, olives, salt, and pepper. Simmer 15 minutes. Place fish in a heated serving dish and pour sauce over. Serves 4.

Hugh Kremer

Clam Fritter Pie

20 chowder clams
2 packages Jiffy cornbread mix
3 eggs
2 Tbs. Texas Pete sauce
1 Tbs. apple cider vinegar
½ cup mayonnaise or sour cream
2 medium onions, minced
½ cup minced sweet peppers
½ cup minced hot peppers

Boil clams in 1 gallon of water over high heat until shells have opened approximately 1". Drain in colander. Rinse with cold water. Remove meat from shells. Meanwhile, combine cornbread mix, eggs, hot sauce, vinegar, and mayonnaise or sour cream. Mix well. Add onions and peppers and squeeze through your fingers until well mixed. Stir in the clams. Place in a large buttered baking dish. Sprinkle with garlic salt. Bake at 350° until golden brown on top. Let rest 10 minutes covered by a dish towel. If clams are not available, try conch.

Charlie Mauldin

Ted's Red Clam Sauce

6 Tbs. olive oil
1 onion, chopped
2 stalks celery, chopped
26-oz. jar of marinara sauce (homemade or store-bought:
    my favorite is "Newman's Own")
½ tsp. basil
½ tsp. oregano
½ tsp. thyme
¼ tsp. cayenne
Black pepper to taste
2 cloves garlic, crushed
1 cup clam juice
½ cup wine (red or white)
2 cups clams, chopped

Sauté onion and celery in 4 Tbs. oil in a heavy, deep saucepan. When vegetables are translucent, add marinara sauce. Add spices and 1 clove garlic. Cook 5 minutes at medium heat. Add clam juice and wine. Cook 20 minutes longer at medium heat, or until sauce is reduced by one-third. Add clams, 2 Tbs. olive oil, and 1 clove garlic. Simmer for 5 minutes and serve over spaghetti, linguine, or fettucine.

Fresh clams or freshly frozen clams and their juice make the tastiest sauce, but canned clams are acceptable. I give quarts of this sauce to friends at Christmas and it's never been known to last till New Year's.

Ted Rosengarten

Striker's Breakfast

6 clams in the shell, preferably salty ones collected in deep
water

Wash clam shells and place in a pan. Put in heated oven
and cook until clams are done. When clams are ready, put
them into a food processor with their juice. Puree. Serve
over grits.

From the crew on Buster's porch

Anthony McKinzie

171

Fried Conch

1-2 conchs, thinly sliced
5-6 eggs, beaten
3 cups seasoned, crushed crackers
1-2 cups vegetable oil

Tenderize meat by beating with a mallet. Dip slices of conch in eggs and cracker crumbs. Fry in hot oil until lightly browned.

Holland Youngman

Turtle Soup

Turtle soup and turtle stew are one and the same, Leah Garrett explains. When she was a child growing up in the Santee River plantation settlement of South Santee, soup was what people today call stew when it was the sole dish served for dinner. Ladled over rice grown on one of the plantations or in her aunt's fields, and threshed at home, or over grits milled from local corn in McClellanville, turtle soup made a filling and delicious meal. "We were glad for it to eat," says Mrs. Garrett, recalling the many children who sat down at the table in her aunt's house. "Weren't anything much left to throw away."

Turtles aren't as plentiful as they were back then, and some people won't eat turtle if a bowl is set in front of them. Mrs. Garrett still cooks turtle soup, but not as frequently as she once did. The difference in cooking today is in the seasonings. Garlic and different kinds of peppers are added to the pot; onions have replaced scallions, but otherwise her recipe has not changed in fifty years. This version omits the garlic, but you can add some if you wish.

Take a yellow-bellied slider with a shell that measures 12" from neck to tail. Cut off the head and let the blood drain. Immerse in boiling water, remove the shell, and peel off the outer layer of skin, which should come off as if you were peeling shrimp. Prepare the feet as you would prepare chicken feet, by cutting off the toes and scrubbing clean. Cut the meat from the body and legs in small pieces and cover with salted water in a large pot. Add chopped celery, carrots, scallions or onions, bell pepper, and hot pepper to taste. Boil till the meat is almost done; add cut-up white potatoes and cook until the potatoes are tender.

If the turtle is a female you may add any eggs that you find at the end of cooking. The small yellow eggs will dissolve, adding a richness to the stew and thickening it. Mrs. Garrett makes a gravy from bacon and flour which she adds to the soup before serving. The gravy thickens the dish and turns it a deeper brown.

An alligator turtle can be used in place of the yellow-bellied slider. The eggs of the alligator turtle are white, Mrs. Garrett reports, and when added to the soup at the end they stay whole.

Daniel Perlmutter

174

How the Spanish Explorers
Used and Preserved Turtles

Meanwhile we caught a great many turtles of immense size, for during four months they flock to the beach to lay their eggs which are consequently found there in great numbers. Like crocodiles they lay them in the sand and there the intense heat of the sun hatches the young turtles. We took off the shells and collecting the fat, reduced it down and filled large earthen jars. We also salted some of the flesh, but it soon spoiled, though when fresh it was very wholesome and excellent eating.

Benzoni, *La Historia del Mondo Nuovo,* 1565, quoted in "Deer Hab Long Foot, Him Run Fas', Cootuh Hab Shawt Foot, Him Trabble Slow," unpublished manuscript by J. C. Marlow.

Steamed Mussels

¼ cup butter or olive oil
6 shallots, chopped
2 cloves garlic, chopped
1/8 tsp. crushed red pepper
3 quarts mussels, well scrubbed
½ cup white wine

Sauté shallots, garlic, and red pepper in olive oil; add mussels and wine. Cook covered over lively heat, 6 to 8 minutes. Agitate the pan to cook mussels evenly, as though you were popping popcorn. Pour into a heated bowl and serve with crusty bread. Serves 4.

Dolores Humphrey

Fried Alligator

A lot of people who live near the coast claim to eat alligator on occasion, but if you want to find someone who fixes it, you'll have to go to South Santee. Gators are plentiful in the dark-water swamps, ponds, and creeks of the old plantation country flooded and drained by the Santee River. In past days, "wild food" such as alligator and turtle were everyday fare. And while country people may be shy about claiming them, they are offered as local delicacies in upscale restaurants in Charleston.

This recipe was provided by Willie Jenkins of South Santee. One of ten children, Willie recalls that his father was the cook in the family. Alligator tail, fried or stewed, was one of his specialties. "People would bring the gator to my daddy and I'd say, 'Oh, we goin to have something now!'"

Use a young alligator if you can get it. Skin the tail and cut away the liver-colored film. The best meat comes from the upper part of the tail, nearest to the back. Cut the white meat into strips or cubes and cover in vinegar. Let sit over night. Pour off the marinade, wash the meat in fresh vinegar, and rinse in cold water. Pat the meat dry. Season it with salt, pepper, paprika, and thyme. Roll the pieces in flour and deep-fry them in vegetable shortening or Wesson oil.

Fried alligator should be eaten with side dishes of lima beans, collard greens, or cabbage. If you like to dip fried food in sauce, use anything that goes with fried fish or fried chicken. If tuna fish can be called chicken-of-the-sea, then alligator is chicken-of-the-swamp.

Eel

Sometimes when you go crabbing you catch an eel. Scald him in boiling water and scrape him good. Skin him, gut him, cut him up. Fry a piece of fat back, stew him up with scallions, pepper, salt. Some people brown flour and make a gravy. Serve it over rice. Tastes just like a catfish.

Margaret German

We skin our eel. You take the head off and you skin it. How I learned to cook eel, we didn't have Accent. We use the onion, pepper, black pepper. Take a little flour or meal and dust it. It's very delicious when you fry it. It's similar to the shark. It's not as high-scented as that shark.

Elizabeth Colleton

Shrimp Crab Casserole

2 lbs. fresh shrimp
1 lb. crabmeat
Sherry to taste (optional)
2 Tbs. butter or margarine
1 4-oz. can sliced mushrooms, drained
2 Tbs. chopped green onions
¼ cup butter or margarine
¼ cup all-purpose flour
2 cups milk
1 tsp. Worcestershire sauce
Dash of Old Bay seasoning
1/8 tsp. salt
1/8 tsp. ground white pepper
1/8 tsp. celery salt
2 egg yolks, lightly beaten
½ cup cracker crumbs

Cook shrimp; peel and devein. Combine shrimp, crabmeat, and sherry. Cover and chill 30 minutes.

Melt 2 Tbs. butter in a large saucepan over medium heat. Add mushrooms and green onions and cook until tender. Remove from heat and set aside. Melt ¼ cup butter in large saucepan; add flour, stirring until smooth. Cook 1 minute. Gradually add milk; cook over medium heat, stirring, until thickened and bubbly. Stir in Worcestershire sauce and seasonings. Stir about a quarter of the hot mixture into yolks, and add to remaining hot mixture while stirring. Stir in mushroom mixture and seafood. Spoon into a lightly greased 13" x 9" x 2" baking dish. Sprinkle with cracker crumbs. Bake at 350° for 20 minutes.

Kathy Leland

Jackie's Seafood Casserole

2 eggs, beaten
1 Tbs. garlic powder
1 tsp. salt
1 Tbs. dillweed
1 tsp. pepper
1 Tbs. parsley
1 Tbs. dry mustard
4 scallions, diced
½ cup mayonnaise
1 tsp. horseradish
2 Tbs. lemon juice
1 cup bread crumbs
1½ lbs. seafood (I use fish, boneless, of course)
5 asparagus spears, fresh or frozen, diced
Paprika

Combine all ingredients and pour into an oiled casserole dish. Top with paprika. Bake at 400° for 30 minutes.

I use fresh herbs if available and double the amounts.

Jackie Morrison, Laurel Hill Bed and Breakfast

Seafood Quesadillas

4 strips bacon
1 onion, diced
1 red bell pepper, diced
1 green bell pepper, diced
1 lb. shrimp, peeled and chopped
"Spike" seasoning
1 lb. fresh crabmeat
Texas Pete hot sauce
Worcestershire sauce
Lemon juice
Mayonnaise
Paul Prudhomme's Seafood Magic
12 flour tortillas
Jack cheese
Salsa
Guacamole
Sour cream

Cook bacon; remove from heat, drain, and crumble. In the drippings, sauté onion, peppers, shrimp, and Spike seasoning. Drain. Mix crabmeat, sauces, lemon juice, and enough mayonnaise to make a paste. Combine shrimp and crabmeat mixtures and add Seafood Magic to taste. Heat tortillas and spread with grated cheese. Add seafood mixture and cover with another tortilla. Top with salsa, guacamole, and sour cream.

Grace Smith, T.W. Graham and Company

Elegant Seafood Casserole

Spray a large casserole dish with non-stick cooking spray and spread deviled crab (see recipes, pp. 130-132) in bottom. Bake at 350° for 10 minutes. Sauté 1 lb. shrimp for 3 to 4 minutes. Sauté 1 lb. scallops for 3 to 4 minutes. Place shrimp and scallops on top of crab, saving juice for white sauce. Make white sauce (see recipe, p. 223) and cover seafood. Spread grated cheddar cheese on top, sparingly. Too much cheese takes away from the seafood flavor. Heat in a moderate oven. Serves 6 to 8.

Shirley McClellan

Seafood Fancy

¾ cup chopped onion
¾ cup chopped bell pepper
1 cup chopped celery
1 cup crabmeat, flaked
1 cup cooked shrimp
Salt and pepper to taste
1 tsp. Worcestershire sauce
1 cup mayonnaise
1 cup soft bread crumbs
2 Tbs. melted butter

Combine vegetables, crabmeat, shrimp, salt, pepper, Worcestershire sauce, and mayonnaise. Put mixture in a greased 1-quart casserole or 8 individual shells. Toss crumbs in butter. Sprinkle over top. Bake at 350° for 30 minutes or until mixture is hot and crumbs are golden brown. Serves 6 to 8.

Margie Leland

Viola Wright's Seafood Pie

1 lb. crabmeat, lump or backfin
2 cups seasoned bread crumbs
½ tsp. dry mustard
2 Tbs. mayonnaise
Dash salt and pepper
½ bell pepper, diced
1 cup chopped scallops
1 cup fresh small shrimp, cleaned
½ can fresh oysters, diced (optional)
Small amount of sweet onion, chopped
Parsley
2 eggs, beaten

Combine all ingredients and mix until moist.

Spoon into a buttered glass pie plate. Bake at 350° for 35 to 40 minutes. Slice in wedges and serve. This mixture can be stuffed inside a whole salmon and baked.

Jenny Hane

Seafood Pie

I love this recipe because a pound of crabmeat can be made to feed eight to ten people.

4 eggs
1 lb. crabmeat, 2 lbs. shrimp, or a combination of the two
1 cup diced celery
1 cup grated cheese
1½ cups mayonnaise
1½ Tbs. Worcestershire sauce
3 Tbs. sherry
Salt and pepper to taste
Crushed crackers

Beat eggs and add all other ingredients. Top with cracker crumbs. Bake 1 hour at 325° or until a knife inserted in the center comes out clean. This dish may be put together ahead and refrigerated. Leave off the crumbs until just before baking, and cook a little longer.

Jackie Morrison, Laurel Hill Bed and Breakfast

Seafood Omelet

1 Tbs. clarified butter or vegetable oil
¼ cup sliced mushrooms
½ cup shrimp, cleaned and deveined
¼ cup crabmeat, picked clean
1 Tbs. clarified butter
4-5 eggs, beaten well
½ cup grated Swiss cheese

Sauté first 4 ingredients in a non-stick omelet pan. Cook until shrimp are just pink. Reserve half of the seafood mixture on a plate for filling.

Add 1 Tbs. clarified butter to the pan. Pour in the beaten eggs. Stir for about 15 seconds, using a plastic spatula to pull the sides of the mass to the middle. Make sure the eggs are not sticking to the pan. Flip the omelet. Add seafood mixture to the center of the omelet along with some grated Swiss cheese. Gently roll the omelet onto a serving plate. Garnish with a few mushrooms, a shrimp, and a sprinkling of cheese.

Jeff Coan

Grilling Seafood

The most important part of grilling any seafood is to pay attention while it cooks. Seafood, like beef, continues to cook for a minute or two when removed from the grill. It is therefore better to slightly undercook it than to overcook it. Marinate or baste with your favorite dressing, oil, or sauce. This will keep your seafood from sticking to the grill. Grilling times will vary according to thickness, whether the shells and skin are on or off, the hotness of the fire, and the distance of the grill from the coals. The following times are approximate; watch what you're doing and keep all the variables in mind. A safe rule is to allow 10 minutes on the grill for every inch of thickness. As soon as fish begins to flake it is ready to come off the grill. You can sprinkle fresh herbs over the coals as you grill to add flavor.

Small whole fish, 6 to 9 minutes per side.

Large whole fish, 11 to 20 minutes per side, longer if thick or stuffed.

Small fillets, such as triggerfish, flounder, sea bass, Spanish mackerel, or any thin fillet, 4 to 8 minutes per side. Turn only if flesh is firm and thick enough to hold together.

Large fish fillets, such as grouper, tile, dolphin, or snapper, and fish steaks, such as tuna, mackerel, swordfish, or shark, 5 minutes per side, longer for very thick pieces.

Kabobs 1 to 1½" thick, 9 to 15 minutes, or about 3 minutes per side.

Large shrimp, 3 to 4 minutes per side.
Medium shrimp, 2 to 3 minutes per side.
Shrimp can be grilled with or without shells. When they turn pink, they are done.

Sea scallops (large), 2 to 3 minutes per side.
Bay scallops (small), 1 to 2 minutes per side.
Scallops are done when they lose their translucence.

Brush soft-shell crabs with melted butter and place over hot coals for 3 minutes. Brush again, turn, and continue cooking, basting, and turning until the crabs are reddish in color.

Bernadette Humphrey

S. Williams

Grilled Fish

2 fish fillets, about 1" thick
1 Tbs. mustard
2 Tbs. red wine
Cracker crumbs

Mix mustard and wine; spread on fish. Broil for 5 minutes, then turn, baste, and broil for 3 more minutes. Sprinkle with cracker crumbs and cook 3 more minutes, or until fish is done. Reduce the broiling time for thinner fillets.

Jackie Morrison, Laurel Hill Bed and Breakfast

Cindy Vaughn shows Katrina Owens how to sew a net.

Accompaniments

I've worked in seafood about twenty-five years—shrimp, crab, fish. I love it. It's an art. I started out with shrimp, heading shrimp, then I worked in the market, cleaning fish, selling it. Picking crab is an art. Long time ago, these crabs that we're picking now, people wouldn't fool with them. These were small stuff. Those crabs were so big and beautiful. When I was a child you could buy a pound of crabmeat for a dollar and thirty-five cents, a pound of shrimp for thirty-nine or forty-nine cents. Claw meat is brown, with a heavier texture. Claw meat is sweeter. The back fin is the flakes from the side—we call that the Special. Your Jumbo Lump comes from the front of the crab's body, the Lump from the back. Right now we got about twenty-one ladies, three packers and seventeen pickers. On a good day we can pack 400 pounds. We can do as much as 500 pounds if I got all my ladies in. We are all like one big family.

Irene Pinckney, Supervisor, South Carolina Crab Company

Cornbread

½ cup oil
2 eggs, or the equivalent egg substitute
1 can cream-style corn
1 8-oz. carton nonfat sour cream or yogurt
2 cups self-rising cornmeal
½ tsp. baking powder

Mix ingredients together and pour into a 9" x 13" x 2" pan sprayed with non-stick cooking spray. Bake at 400° for 30 minutes.

Suzanne Britt

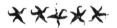

A leaf rasps
down a tin roof and falls
a boat for sale

Sam Savage, *Eighteen Kinds of Loneliness*

Mae's Cornbread

1 2/3 cups self-rising flour
2 cups cornmeal
2 eggs, beaten
3 Tbs. shortening
3 Tbs. sugar
1½ tsp. salt
2 cups milk

Mix ingredients together and beat until smooth. You might have to add a little more milk. Pour into a 9" x 13" pan. Bake at 350° for 30 to 45 minutes. This recipe makes a very moist cornbread.

Mae Hutto

Fresh Herb Scones

Great with chowders and seafood salads.

2 cups flour
1 Tbs. sugar
¼ cup chopped fresh parsley
1 Tbs. chopped fresh thyme or 1 tsp. dried thyme
3 tsp. baking powder
1 tsp. chopped fresh rosemary or ¼ tsp. dried rosemary
      leaves, crushed
½ tsp. salt
1/3 cup butter or margarine
½ cup milk
1 egg, slightly beaten

Heat oven to 400°. Lightly grease a cookie sheet. Combine flour, sugar, parsley, thyme, baking powder, rosemary, and salt. Using a pastry blender or fork, cut in butter until the mixture resembles coarse crumbs. Stir in milk and egg just until moistened. On a floured surface, gently knead dough 10 times. Place on cookie sheet; pat dough into a 6" circle. Cut into 8 wedges; separate slightly. Bake at 400° for 15 to 20 minutes, or until brown.

Cathy Woods

Shrimp Hushpuppies

1 cup Autrey's hushpuppy mix
2/3 cup water
Small shrimp or shrimp pieces
Grated onion

Combine hushpuppy mix and water until well blended. Add grated onion and shrimp and mix again. Let mixture stand about 5 minutes. Mix and drop by tablespoons into 375° oil. Fry 3 minutes or until golden brown. Makes about 20 puppies.

Wanda Cumbee

Lydia Sisson

Hoover's Hushpuppies

From the beginning of my memory, Hoover's Mill and Wright's Creek were the center of our lives. My grandparents, Ruby and B.T. Hoover, had both worked as welders at the shipyard in Panama City during World War II and used all they made, $4,000, to buy the old mill straddling the creek in Holmes County, Florida. Daddy thought it would be a better investment than gulf-front property for $5.00 an acre because he couldn't grow anything in the sand.

They started with two sets of "rocks" run by a wheel set in the creek, and expanded to six over the years. At one time or another, everyone in the family worked in the mill. Everyone in the family learned to swim in that creek, too. My mother said that when they moved to the mill, my granddaddy threw all four kids in the middle of the creek and hollered, "Swim." He said he had too much to do to worry about them drowning all the time. So they swam. We all did. And we ground cornmeal. They still do.

This recipe is as close as I can come to the hushpuppy mix my family makes. I asked for the original and they gave it to me based on 400 pounds of cornmeal.

1 cup white cornmeal
1 tsp. flour
¼ tsp. baking powder
½ tsp. salt
1 pinch baking soda

¼ cup milk
Up to 1 cup of water, beer, or Ro-Tel tomatoes
1 medium onion, chopped fine

Mix all the dry ingredients. Then add the liquid and onion and mix until the batter is the consistency of mashed potatoes. Use a spoon to drop the hushpuppies into hot peanut oil. Brown on both sides.

Donna Stoudenmire

Good Hushpuppies

2 cups seafood breader
1 onion, diced
1 can cream-style corn
Black pepper to taste
2 eggs
Evaporated milk

Mix seafood breader, onion, corn, and black pepper. Add eggs and enough milk to make a creamy batter. Drop by tablespoonsful into hot oil. Fry until golden brown.

Sara Nell Scott

Mother's Biscuits

My grandmother cooked "dinner" every day for a crowd, usually five to ten family members, the "mill hands," and a few friends or neighbors who straggled in about lunch time. She made huge pots and platters of vegetables, stews, roasts, gravies, fried fish and meats, and always cornbread or biscuits or both. I've tried all my life to make her biscuits. This is how she did it. If you're lucky, with practice, you'll come fairly close. I'm still working on it.

Preheat your oven to 400°. Sift self-rising flour into a large bowl, almost to the top. Then push the flour out and up with the backs of your fingers, forming a "well." What you have is a thick bowl made of flour inside the real bowl. Fill the flour well almost to the top with buttermilk. Pour some peanut oil into a "baker" (I use a seasoned cast-iron frying pan.) Coat the pan and pour the excess into the buttermilk.

At this point, you're probably wondering about ratios. My grandmother never would say. I use approximately 1 Tbs. oil to 1 cup of buttermilk. Start stirring the milk around with two fingers, knocking a little flour from the well. Continue this very gradually, picking up flour, until it becomes a soft dough. By now you should have your hand in it. The dough should be separating easily from the dry flour.

Now, scoot your fingers up under the edge of the dough, digging slightly into the well, and fold part of it over into itself. Pat it down firmly with your knuckles. If your hand

gets gooey, coat it with flour. With your other hand, turn the bowl a quarter turn. Repeat this until the dough starts to spring back gently after being punched down. This process adds more flour and stiffens the dough. Flour your hands and pinch off a biscuit between your thumb and forefinger, roll it around in your hands to smooth it out and make it round. Place it in the pan and then flip it over gently. This takes excess grease from the pan and coats the top for browning. Fill the pan with biscuits, then pat them down so that they touch on all sides. Bake until golden.

Donna Stoudenmire

Fig Marmalade

Chop fresh figs or leave whole, as desired. Slice 2 lemons and boil until tender. Drain juice. For 2 lbs. of figs, use about 2 Tbs. sugar. Grate 2 oranges, using pulp, rind, and juice. Add cooked lemons. Cook all together until figs are tender and juice passes the "jelly test."

Penn Gregg, Millbrook Plantation

Onion Kuchen

3 Tbs. butter
2 medium onions, peeled and cut into rings
1 10-roll package refrigerated buttermilk or homestyle
    biscuits
1 egg
1 8-oz. package sour cream
½ tsp. salt
Pinch black pepper
1 tsp. poppy seeds

Melt butter in frying pan. Sauté onions until just soft. Separate biscuits. Place in a single layer in an ungreased 8" layer cake pan or square baking pan. Press together to cover bottom of pan completely. Spoon onion rings over biscuits.

Beat egg, then blend in sour cream, salt, and pepper. Pour over onions and spread evenly. Sprinkle with poppy seeds. Bake 30 minutes in a 375° oven. Slice into wedges. Serve hot or cold. Serves 4 to 6.

Ruth Edwards

Dry Shelly Rice

When some people cook rice, you got to scrape it off the spoon. Dry shelly rice don't stick to nothing.

I got two secrets. See the second ring on your finger, second joint? Put your rice in the pot, level it off. Put your finger on top of the rice, and put in the water up to that second ring. Let it boil right on down, and when the water's just about gone, put the cover on, turn the fire down, and just let it soak. Dry shelly rice.

Charles Williams

Red Rice

My red rice is cooked red. Put your meat in there.   Take a quarter cup of vegetable oil, add a half a can of tomato paste, and fill the cup up with water. All your liquid goes together. Put the cap on the pot. Course you got to stir it, 'cause of that tomato. Tomato burns easy.

Charles Williams

T.W. Graham Red Rice

3 strips bacon
1 onion, chopped
1 bell pepper, chopped
1 can tomato paste
Salt and pepper
Seasoning salt (we like to use "Spike")
1 fresh sausage link, cooked and crumbled
3 cups cooked rice

Cook bacon and remove from the pan. Sauté pepper and onion in drippings. Drain excess grease. Add remaining ingredients; heat and serve.

Sherry Browne, T.W. Graham and Company

Carole's Tabouli

1 cup bulgur wheat
1/3 cup olive oil
1 Tbs. lemon juice (add more later to taste)
1 cucumber, finely chopped
2 medium tomatoes, finely chopped
1 cup chopped fresh parsley
½ cup chopped fresh mint (optional)

Prepare bulgur wheat according to package directions. Add other ingredients and mix. Chill at least 1 hour. Great served as a salad on a bed of lettuce with seafood, or as a sandwich in a pita pocket.

Carole Hill

Squash Casserole

1½ lbs. squash
1 medium onion, chopped
6 saltine crackers, crushed
½ cup mayonnaise
2 beaten eggs
1 package Hidden Valley Ranch dressing mix
½ cup grated cheese

Topping:
8 Ritz crackers, crumbled
½ stick butter or margarine, melted

Boil squash and onion in a small amount of water until tender; drain. Mix with other ingredients and pour into casserole. Mix cracker crumbs and butter; sprinkle over the top. Bake at 300° for 30 minutes.

Priscilla M. Parker

Stuffed Collards

12 large collard leaves
1 lb. ground lamb or beef
2 large onions, finely minced
½ cup chopped fresh parsley
¼ cup uncooked rice
¼ cup chopped fresh basil
Juice of ½ lemon
1/3 cup tomato sauce
Salt and pepper to taste
2 Tbs. butter or margarine
1 cup sour cream
¼ cup chunky salsa

Place collard leaves in a large container and pour boiling water over them to cover; soak until supple. Drain and pat dry with paper towels. Mix meat, onions, parsley, rice, basil, lemon juice, tomato sauce, salt, and pepper. Divide meat mixture equally onto collard leaves from which you have removed the tough stems. Roll up and fold the sides to form a package. Tie with cord. Brown collard rolls in melted butter on all sides. Remove from pan and place in a single layer in a lightly greased casserole dish. Add about ¼ cup hot water to the pan in which the rolls were browned. Pour over collard rolls. Cover and bake in a preheated 350° oven for 1½ hours. Mix sour cream and salsa and pour over cooked rolls. Return uncovered to oven to heat through. Serves 4.

Dewey G. Williams, Jr.

Corn Casserole

1 stick margarine
1 onion, cut up fine
1 bell pepper, cut up fine
Dash each of salt and pepper
4 to 5 tsp. flour
2 cans cream-style corn
1 cup milk
1 cup Ritz crackers, crushed

Melt ½ stick of margarine in a frying pan over low heat. Add onion and bell pepper, salt, pepper, and flour. Then add corn and milk. Turn off heat. In another pan over low heat, blend ½ stick margarine and cracker crumbs. Turn off heat, pour corn mixture into casserole dish. Sprinkle with cracker crumbs. Bake at 350° until brown.

Mae Hutto

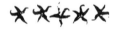

Returning trawler—
in a net by the wheelhouse
onions, potatoes

Sam Savage, *Trawlers*

Broccoli Casserole

2 packages frozen chopped broccoli
2 eggs
1 stick margarine
1 small onion, chopped
1 can cream of mushroom soup
½ cup mayonnaise
Salt and pepper to taste
1 cup grated cheese
10 to 15 Ritz crackers, crushed

Cook broccoli until tender; drain. Combine eggs, margarine, onion, soup, mayonnaise, salt, and pepper in a large casserole dish. Top with cheese and cracker crumbs and bake about 40 minutes at 350°.

Mae Hutto

Tipsy Carrots

Good with fish.

1 lb. carrots, peeled and cut diagonally into "coins"
2 Tbs. butter
2 Tbs. honey
½ cup Amber rum (or substitute ½ to 1 Tbs. rum extract
        mixed with ¼ cup water)
1/8 tsp. nutmeg
½ tsp. cinnamon
Salt and pepper

Cook carrots for 8 minutes. Drain well. Add remaining ingredients and toss to coat carrots. Place in *hot* serving dish. Serves 4.

Ruth Edwards

Sweet Potato Soufflé

1 lb. sweet potatoes
1 cup sugar
1 stick margarine
2 eggs, beaten well
½ tsp. salt
1 to 2 tsp. vanilla
Cinnamon to taste
1 small can crushed pineapple
½ cup raisins
2 tsp. honey
1 cup marshmallows

Mix the first 7 ingredients with the electric mixer, then add raisins, pineapple, and honey. Put in a casserole dish. Bake at 350° for 30 to 35 minutes. Top with marshmallows and sprinkle with cinnamon. Return to oven and allow marshmallows to brown.

Mae Hutto

Summer Squash Loaf

1 lb. summer squash, either yellow crookneck or zucchini
3 eggs, lightly beaten
½ cup finely minced onion
¼ cup shredded cheddar cheese
¼ cup milk
2 Tbs. flour
½ tsp. salt
¼ tsp. pepper

Cook cubed or sliced unpeeled squash in boiling water until tender. Drain in fine-meshed colander or sieve until all liquid is removed. Pulverize with a potato masher. Do not use a blender or electric mixer. Thoroughly mix squash, egg, onion, cheese, milk, flour, salt, and pepper. Pour into lightly greased 8½" x 4½" x 2½" loaf pan. Cover with foil. Put in shallow baking dish and add enough hot water to come up about 2" around loaf pan. Bake in preheated 350° oven for about 45 minutes or until a knife inserted in the center comes out clean. Let cool on a wire rack 20 minutes. Invert loaf onto serving platter. Slice and garnish each portion with a teaspoon of drained diced pimientos and a sprig of fresh basil. Serves 6.

Dewey G. Williams, Jr.

Zucchini Bread

6 cups chopped zucchini, drained
5 cups flour
4 cups sugar
2 cups oil
6 eggs, beaten well
½ box raisins (about 2 cups)
2 Tbs. vanilla
3 tsp. cinnamon, or to taste
1 Tbs. salt

Mix all together. If mixture is too dry, add a little more oil. Fill 3 or 4 loaf pans, greased and floured. Bake at 350° until brown, about 30 minutes.

Icing

1 box powdered sugar
1 stick margarine
1 4-oz. package cream cheese
1 Tbs. vanilla

Blend with mixer and spread on top of cooled bread. Loaves can be frozen to eat later.

Mae Hutto

Black Bean and Corn Salad

Adding brown rice makes a complete protein, stretches the recipe, and tastes great. I serve this in a shallow bowl surrounded by chunks of ripe avocado. It is pretty and so good, and can be made into a low fat dish by omitting the avocado and reducing the oil to ½ Tbs.

2 cups black beans, cooked and drained, or 2-3 cans, rinsed
    and drained
1 green bell pepper, chopped
1 red bell pepper, chopped
1 yellow bell pepper, chopped
1 purple onion or 1 cup green onion, chopped
1 cup fresh, frozen, or canned white kernel corn
½ cup chopped cilantro
1-2 cups cooked brown rice (optional)
2 cups plum tomatoes, chopped

Dressing:
2 Tbs. wine or Balsamic vinegar
2 tsp. cumin
2 Tbs. olive oil
2 Tbs. fresh lime juice
Salt, pepper, red pepper flakes

Dress the salad about 1 hour before serving and let it stand to reach room temperature. Serves 6 to 8.

Penn Gregg, Millbrook Plantation

Sauerkraut Salad

1 27-oz. jar sauerkraut, drained
1½ cups finely chopped celery
¾ cup finely chopped sweet onion
1 carrot, grated
½ bell pepper, chopped
½ red pepper, chopped
1 cup sugar
½ cup salad oil
½ cup white vinegar
1 tsp. celery seed

Combine sauerkraut, celery, onion, carrot, and peppers.
Dissolve sugar in oil and vinegar. Add celery seed. Pour
over vegetables and toss. Cover and chill for several hours.
Drain before serving and place on a bed of lettuce.

Dot Best

Rocky Mount Slaw

1 medium head of cabbage
1 Tbs. celery seed
1 tsp. salt
½ tsp. pepper
1/3 cup sugar
1 tsp. dry mustard
1 Tbs. turmeric
2 Tbs. white vinegar
1 Tbs. salad oil

Shred cabbage and put in bowl. Add celery seed, salt, and pepper. Mix well. Put sugar, mustard, turmeric, white vinegar, and salad oil in a small saucepan and bring to a boil. Turn off heat and let cool. Add dressing to cabbage and mix thoroughly. This slaw will keep for at least a week in the refrigerator. If cabbage is large, make a second turn* of dressing.

Suzanne Britt

The word "turn" is used locally to mean a batch or recipe.

Pantry Coleslaw

1½ cups plus 2 Tbs. mayonnaise
6 Tbs. plus 1 tsp. sugar
3 Tbs. plus ½ tsp. wine vinegar
¾ cup plus 1 Tbs. oil
1/8 tsp. each of garlic, onion, mustard, and celery powders
Dash of black pepper
1 Tbs. plus 2 tsp. lemon juice
¾ cup plus 1 Tbs. half-and-half
½ tsp. salt
2 heads of cabbage, very finely shredded

Blend together mayonnaise, sugar, vinegar, and oil. Add the spice powders, pepper, lemon juice, half-and-half, and salt. Stir until smooth. Pour over coleslaw in a large bowl and toss until cabbage is well coated. The dressing keeps well, covered tightly, in the refrigerator for several days.

Dave Mandeville

Tomato Gravy

Heat a couple of tablespoons of drippings or oil in a frying pan. Add flour and brown slightly to make a roux. Then, add a quart or so of tomatoes, canned or fresh, and stir until thickened. Salt and pepper to taste. Make this while your biscuits cook, and simmer it until they're done. This is delicious with fish and grits.

Donna Stoudenmire

Selden Baker Hill

Tomato Dumplings

1 cup finely chopped onion
1 cup finely chopped bell or Anaheim chile peppers
½ cup finely chopped celery
4 Tbs. butter or margarine
1 bay leaf
1 28-oz. can chopped tomatoes
1 Tbs. brown sugar
4 Tbs. finely minced fresh basil
½ tsp. salt
½ tsp. pepper
1 cup flour
½ tsp. salt
1½ tsp. baking powder
1 Tbs. *cold* butter or margarine
4 Tbs. finely minced fresh parsley
2/3 cup milk

Sauté onion, pepper, and celery in butter until tender. Add bay leaf, tomatoes with liquid, brown sugar, basil, salt and pepper. Cover. Simmer 10 minutes. Combine flour, baking powder, and salt. Cut in butter. Add milk and parsley and stir until just mixed. Drop by tablespoonfuls into 6 mounds into tomato mixture. Cover and simmer 15 minutes, or until toothpick inserted in one of the dumplings comes out clean. Remove bay leaf and serve in soup plates. Garnish with fresh basil leaves. Makes a complete light supper with salad and bread. Serves 6.

Dewey G. Williams, Jr.

Summer Porch

Catch the morning breeze.
Taste the tang of it.
Listen for the sound of a screen door
banging the outs-and-ins
of small children running
down to the beach.

See the kaleidoscope of wet suits
hanging out with gulls
on the rails
and window sills encrusted
with oyster shells, sandollars
and angel wings.

Hear the creak of the hammock
and porch swing.
Fill the lazy afternoon
with books, naps
and a tinkling pitcher of lemonade.

After supper
when the first star appears,
huddle up close to the creepiness
of old tales
told after the moon is down
and lights are out.

Irene Nuite Lofton, *From My Mother's Porch.*

Sherry Browne's Tartar Sauce

5 cups dill pickles with their juice (do not use sweet or
    kosher pickles)
2½ cups strong white onions
2 carrots
Mayonnaise

Put the pickles and their juice in a blender. Puree. Dump
into a colander. Put the onions and carrots in the blender
and puree. Add to the pickles and mix well; allow to drain
until all juice is removed. Place in a bowl and mix with
enough mayonnaise to form a paste.

T.W. Graham and Company

Dipping Sauces

(1) Combine equal amounts of soy or tamari sauce and
freshly squeezed lemon juice, and add a dash of water.
Add crushed garlic and/or grated ginger root to taste.

(2) Combine ½ cup catsup and 2 heaping Tbs. white
horseradish.

Dale Rosengarten

Seafood Marinade

¼ cup catsup
¼ cup oil
1 tsp. Worcestershire sauce
2 tsp. hickory smoke
2 Tbs. vinegar
½ tsp. dry mustard
½ tsp. salt
½ tsp. pepper
Hot sauce to taste

Mix all ingredients and use to marinate fish, shrimp, or other seafoods.

Bobbie Davis

Garlic Butter Sauce

Great for dipping and as a sauce for grilling seafood, especially large shrimp and soft shell crabs.

8 oz. butter
4 Tbs. olive oil
2 cloves garlic, freshly minced.

Slowly melt butter. Stir in garlic and oil; heat 4 minutes.

Bernadette Humphrey

Béchamel Sauce

2 Tbs. butter
3 Tbs. flour
¼ tsp. salt
Dash of cayenne pepper (optional)
2 cups hot milk

Melt butter in a saucepan; stir in flour. Cook slowly over low heat, stirring constantly, until the roux bubbles and foams for about 3 minutes. It will be slightly golden but should not brown. Remove from heat. Add salt, cayenne, and milk. Stir rapidly with a wooden spoon. Cook over medium heat, stirring constantly, until sauce bubbles. Cook 1 minute longer. Makes 2 cups.

Adam Howard

Holland Youngman

White Sauce

4 Tbs. butter
4 Tbs. flour
½ tsp. salt
½ tsp. white pepper
2 cups milk

Melt butter in a saucepan over low heat. Blend in flour, salt, and pepper. Add milk. Stir constantly with a wire whisk until mixture thickens.

Shirley McClellan

Hollandaise Sauce

3 egg yolks
4 Tbs. boiling water
1½ Tbs. lemon juice
½ cup butter, melted
½ tsp. salt
Dash cayenne pepper

Place the egg yolks in the top of a double boiler over—not in—hot water. Cook and beat with a wire whisk until they begin to thicken. Add the water by tablespoonfuls and beat until you have incorporated it all. Beat in lemon juice. Remove from heat. Continue beating while adding the melted butter, salt, and pepper. Beat until sauce is thick.

Dale Rosengarten

Desserts

Our village lies along the bend of a creek, and curls around the shrimp docks like a mother cat around nursing kittens. Visitors who drive through here are enchanted with the old-fashioned quaintness of the quiet streets shaded by enormous trees, the old houses with large yards, the unhurried, peaceful appearance of the entire place. Former inhabitants who come back for brief visits invariably exclaim, "The village never changes." But it does change. The village is different in a good many ways from the place it was when I came here just before Pearl Harbor.

Sally Graham Vann, August 18, 1960

Sally's Ice Cream

You can't have a summer seafood dinner without having home-churned peach ice cream for dessert, can you? This recipe was given to me by Sally Graham Vann.

4 eggs
1½ cups sugar (I use about half that)
1 large can evaporated milk (I substitute cream)
1½ qts. whole milk, scalded
3 Tbs. vanilla
Dash of salt
Peaches to taste, peeled, cut up, and sweetened with sugar
      or steeped in peach schnapps or other liqueur

Make a custard by whipping the eggs until frothy, adding sugar and whole milk and cooking over low heat (a double boiler is safest), stirring almost constantly until the mixture coats the spoon thinly. If evaporated milk is used, add it at this point. Continue cooking until it coats the spoon moderately (a thin custard). If using cream, add it at this point. Let cool. Pour custard into chilled churn container. Churn until blades begin to "tug" on the sides of the container, then add peaches. Churn until you think it's ready, then churn 10 minutes more. This will feed as many people as you have on your front porch, whatever the number.

Karen Shuler

I was a confirmed milk drinker when I moved to the village, but no dairy delivered milk here. For a year or so, I drank tea and coffee. Eventually I found someone with a cow and a willing spirit, and we had a very agreeable arrangement. I would put an empty bottle outside, with a poker chip on the top. The owner of the cow, after milking, would wander over to my house and leave me a bottle of milk and take the empty bottle and the poker chip. When he had collected a pile of poker chips, he would take them to my husband, who would pay him the agreed price per quart for each poker chip.

Then for a time there was a small dairy that operated here. It must have been in the summer, because what I recall most vividly is the sour milk. The person delivering the milk would race madly from the dairy to the village, sounding a loud horn at the home of each customer. You would rush out to the car, snatch up your milk, and speed it straight into your refrigerator, still warm from the cows. And then, when it got cold and you tried to drink it, it would be sour. I don't know why, but that's the way I remember it.

Now, of course, things are different. Dairy trucks bring their wares here and we buy dairy products from the grocery store.

Sally Graham Vann, August 18, 1960

Crispy Cobbler

1/3 cup butter
1 cup sifted flour
1 cup sugar
2 tsp. double-acting baking powder
1/8 tsp. salt
¾ cup milk
4 cups fresh or frozen berries or rhubarb, or canned or fresh
    sliced peaches or apricots

Place butter in an 8" x 10" x 2" baking pan. Place in a warm oven to melt the butter. Sift together the flour, sugar, baking powder, and salt. Stir in the milk and blend until smooth. Turn into the baking pan, over the melted butter. Spread with the fruit. Bake in a 375° oven for 40 minutes. Serve with cream or half-and-half.

If desired, the fruit can be placed in the pan over the melted butter, and the topping poured over the fruit.

Dale Rosengarten

Peach Cobbler

This is my mother-in-law's recipe. I have substituted local blueberries and/or pears with great success.
Martha Zierden

2 cups sliced peaches
1 cup sugar
1 cup self-rising flour
1 cup milk
1 stick (½ cup) butter

Heat oven to 350°. Melt butter in a glass baking dish; pour half aside in a measuring cup. Arrange fruit in glass dish in remaining butter. Mix the milk, sugar, and flour together; pour loosely over fruit. Drizzle remaining butter over the top. Bake 1 hour or until golden brown.

Lula M. Stroman

Pig Lickin' Cake
(Mandarin Orange Cake)

1 18-oz. box butter yellow Duncan Hines Cake Mix
¾ cup cooking oil
4 eggs
1 11-oz. can mandarin oranges and juice

Beat all ingredients together for 4 minutes. Pour into greased cake pans. Bake at 350° for 20 to 25 minutes. The layers will be thin. This cake is best done in 3 layers but it may be baked in only 2 layers or in a tube pan, in which case cooking time should be longer. Cool and ice.

Icing:
1 small box instant vanilla pudding mix
1 15½-oz. can crushed pineapple, undrained
1 9-oz. container whipped topping, thawed

Mix all ingredients by hand. Do not use an electric mixer. Iced cake is best kept refrigerated. Keeps well.

This icing recipe could be used on almost any cake. It is delicious and stays moist.

Dot Best

Pecan Pie

4 eggs
2 cups sugar
2 Tbs. flour
2 Tbs. water
3 Tbs. vinegar
1 stick butter, melted
1 cup chopped pecans

Combine all ingredients and place in an unbaked pie shell. Bake for 1 hour at 300°.

Priscilla M. Parker

Fudge Pie

½ cup butter
3 squares unsweetened baking chocolate
4 beaten eggs
1½ cups sugar
¼ tsp. salt
3 Tbs. corn syrup
1 tsp. vanilla
Pie crust

Melt chocolate and butter together in a saucepan. Beat eggs with sugar, salt, corn syrup, and vanilla. Mix together with chocolate butter. Pour into pie shell. Bake about 40 minutes at 350°. Best served with whipped cream.

Martha Zierden

Key Lime Pie

1 cup sugar
¼ cup flour
3 Tbs. cornstarch
¼ tsp. salt
2 cups water
3 egg yolks, beaten
1 Tbs. butter
¼ cup fresh or bottled key lime juice
Rind of 1 lemon or lime, grated
9" pie shell, baked
3 egg whites
¼ tsp. cream of tartar
6 Tbs. sugar

Combine sugar, flour, cornstarch, and salt in a saucepan and stir in the water a tablespoon at a time. Cook, stirring constantly, until thickened. Gradually stir the mixture into the beaten egg yolks; return to low heat and cook, stirring constantly, 2 minutes. Stir in the butter, lime juice, and rind and cool slightly. Pour into the baked pie crust and cool. In a clean bowl, beat egg whites until light and frothy. Add the cream of tartar and continue beating until the whites hold a peak. Gradually beat in the sugar and continue until meringue is stiff and glossy. Pile on cooled pie filling, spreading so it touches the edges of the pie shell. Bake at 425° until the top is brown, 5 to 6 minutes.

Bernadette Humphrey

Chocolate Cheesecake

Rich and easy—a chocolate lover's delight.

1 recipe pie crust dough
1 8-oz. package semi-sweet chocolate chips
½ cup dark rum or water
1 lb. cream cheese, regular or low fat
1 pint sour cream, regular or low fat
½ cup sugar
½ cup flour
6 eggs

Using any pie crust recipe, line a springform pan with crust. Prick bottom with a fork. Bake 10 minutes in a 350° oven.

Melt chocolate with rum or water in top of double boiler; stir until smooth. Combine in a mixing bowl the cheese, sour cream, sugar, flour, and chocolate mixture. Beat until smooth. Add, while continuing to beat, 1 egg at a time. Beat until well blended. Pour into pastry crust and bake at 350° for 45 minutes. Turn off oven and leave cake inside another 30 minutes. Cool to room temperature and refrigerate before serving.

Cynthia Kephart

Uncle Hepburn's Last Voyage

Uncle Hepburn died at ninety-three, having outlived most of his contemporaries, and his descendants accorded him a funeral touched with quiet sadness and deep pride.

But his retirement as a plantation supervisor thirteen years earlier had posed a problem for his family. Then the old man was strong, bright-eyed, and full of energy. He had no idea of rocking away his remaining days on the piazza.

A grandson gave in and bought him his heart's desire, a small shrimp boat. With a helper, Uncle Hepburn put happily to sea.

The first season he made expenses and a little bit more. Winter came. He switched over to oyster picking from an open row boat, but he could hardly wait for the shrimp to run again.

His striker that second season was inexperienced, so Uncle Hepburn told him to hold the wheel while he walked to the aft deck to feed out the net. As the shrimp boat putt-putted through the waves, the net drifted back, ropes snaking out between it and the stern.

Suddenly Uncle Hepburn felt his ankle seized as though by an iron fist. He had stepped into a loop in the rope. It could tighten and cut his foot off, or drag him into the sea and drown him.

The old man took quick action. He dived into the choppy water, gaining enough slack on the rope to slip his ankle out of the deadly trap. He struggled to the surface for air—the whole thing had happened so fast he had had no time to take a deep breath.

His head pressed against the net, which by then had ballooned out in fishing position behind the boat. The thrust of the water swept him inexorably back toward the "bag," a sack of heavy netting into which the catch funnels.

At the toe of the bag Uncle Hepburn doubled over, put his hands together, and stuck his fingers through the mesh. In one smooth powerful effort, into which he put somehow not only the muscles of his arms but those of his back, chest, and legs, he pulled his hands apart. The strong cords gave way to stronger sinew, hardened by eighty years of saw-milling, farming, and fishing, and a rent opened up, big enough for him to slip through.

The striker had thrown the engine out of gear, so when Uncle Hepburn popped to the surface, wheezing like a porpoise, his boat was no more than a few hundred yards away. Swimming powerfully, he just made it to the rail, directed the frightened youngster to lash a rope around him—then fainted, and fell back into the sea. Somehow the striker managed to pull him to the deck.

That night, after hearing his grandfather tell the story, a grandson pulled the boat up on a mud bank, doused it with gasoline, and struck a match.

Jay Shuler, October 3, 1971, from *Snakes in the Outhouse, and Other Causes for Wonder* (McClellanville Arts Council, 1994).

Prayer

There is the open sky
Marsh-tinted at its rim
The quiet lapping of the tide
With the rhythm of a hymn.

The sky above is filled
With clouds of a different hue
And underneath a marsh-green world
Forever old and new.

Mary Evelyn "Teen" Lofton, *Verses at Random*

Beau Bryant Evans

Index

Index

Index

Index

Index

Jenny Hane's SAIL class, St. James-Santee Elementary School. Back row, left to right: Lydia Sisson, Katrina Owens, Carlin Rosengarten, Courtnay Coan, Holland Youngman. Seated, front: Bryan Ruth

Bernadette Humphrey

Order Form

Name_____

Address_____

City_____

State_____Zip_____

Please send me the following:

_____*The McClellanville Coast* Seafood *Cookbook*

_____*The McClellanville Coast Cookbook*

_____*The Visible Village: A McClellanville Scrapbook,
1865-1945* , by William P. Baldwin

_____*Snakes in the Outhouse, and Other Causes for
Wonder*, by Jay Shuler

Each book, $14.95.

Shipping and handling: $3 for up to 4 books; $1 for each
additional book.

I enclose $_____

Please make checks payable to the McClellanville Arts
Council and mail to PO Box 594, McClellanville, SC 29458.

Call (803) 887-3157 for information about bulk orders.